SECOND EDITION

55 SUCCESSFUL HARVARD LAW SCHOOL APPLICATION ESSAYS

What Worked for Them Can Help You Get into the Law School of Your Choice

With Analysis by the Staff of

The Harvard Crimson

ST. MARTIN'S GRIFFIN ⚲ NEW YORK

55 SUCCESSFUL HARVARD LAW SCHOOL APPLICATION ESSAYS: SECOND EDITION. Copyright © 2014 by *The Harvard Crimson*. All rights reserved. Printed in the United States of America. For information, address St. Martin's Press, 175 Fifth Avenue, New York, N.Y. 10010.

www.stmartins.com

Library of Congress Cataloging-in-Publication Data

55 successful harvard law school application essays, second edition: with analysis by the staff of the harvard crimson / The Staff of the Harvard Crimson.—Second edition.
   pages cm
  ISBN 978-1-250-04723-6 (paperback)
  ISBN 978-1-4668-4759-0 (e-book)
  1. Law schools—United States—Admission. 2. Harvard Law School—Admission. 3. College applications—United States. 4. Essay—Authorship. 5. Exposition (Rhetoric) 6. Academic writing. I. Harvard crimson. II. Title: Fifty-five successful Harvard law School application essays.
  KF285.A15 2014
  340.071'17444—dc23

2014008570

St. Martin's Griffin books may be purchased for educational, business, or promotional use. For information on bulk purchases, please contact Macmillan Corporate and Premium Sales Department at 1-800-221-7945, extension 5442, or write specialmarkets@macmillan.com.

First Edition: July 2007
Second Edition: July 2014

D 13 12 11

CONTENTS

INSPIRATION

ACKNOWLEDGMENTS

We at *The Harvard Crimson* would like to thank all who helped assemble the second edition of this book, including: Samir Gupta, David Liu, and LuShuang Xu, who all spearheaded this book's logistics side along with our business manager, Andrew Creamer; Brian Cronin, head of content for the book; Maya Jonas-Silver, who kickstarted the essay review process; Matt Martz of St. Martin's Press for his guidance and thoughtful edits; the fifty-five Harvard Law students who donated essays so that this book's readers might follow their footsteps; and of course the *Crimson*'s editors who penned reviews and ensured this book lived up to the professionalism and quality of our daily, journalistic content.

INTRODUCTION

When the first edition of this book was released in 2007, a swelling applicant pool marked the primary pressure facing law school applicants. At the time the volume of applications was on its way toward record highs, and enrollment still remains above its 2007 levels, but the elevated competition doesn't end with a letter of admission. The class of 2007 entered a job market to find a 92 percent employment rate for law school graduates. For the class of 2012, the most recent available data set when this book was written, that number dropped to 84 percent, tied for second lowest since 1985. Many students sought shelter in law schools during the recession, a factor that has only increased the employment bottleneck in the downturn's wake. And the change hasn't been restricted to quantity. The composition of those jobs has changed, too. In 2007, over three-quarters of graduates found jobs requiring bar passage, i.e., the sort of jobs students attend law school to pursue. For the class of 2012, under two-thirds met that standard. Still more grimly, a mere 56 percent—barely half—found full-time, long-term employment. As recently as the class of 2010 (as far back as the American Bar Association's data extends), that number stood at 70 percent. In today's environment, the premium has risen sharply for the law schools that are still adept at connecting students with future goals. And by extension, the competition for acceptance to those schools has risen, too. In that stark light, the value of an outstanding application to those schools is more vital than ever.

With an application deadline looming, those numbers and pressures might overwhelm you. But don't throw your hands and the book that's in them into the air just yet. Keep reading.

Yes, the application is vital, and no, it isn't effortless, but it offers an excellent opportunity. The law school application brings together several revealing but imperfect glimpses at who you are. Your LSAT score, transcript, résumé, and recommendations all illuminate various aspects of the whole. Your LSAT score points to your reasoning ability and your law school geared skillset with a single, standardized number for helpful comparison across schools. Important as it is, it certainly doesn't secure admission. At most of the top law schools, 25 percent or more of students have LSAT scores below 170. And many reject students with scores well above that. The transcript and résumé both indicate prior experience and success. But the meaning behind college GPA figures varies widely from school to school, and even more so across majors and classes. And a range of unseen circumstances, from personal life to extracurriculars, can affect it from semester to semester. Reliance on a single number risks myopia. The résumé touches on your more substantive experiences, but its succinctness saps them of context and meaning. Recommendations begin the vital task of connecting, of drawing together the far-flung strands of academics, motivation, and who you are. Yet they, too, offer only partial snapshots—of you in a single class or subject, and strictly through the lens of the writer.

None of these components amount to enough on their own. No one part is. But you do have a chance—one chance—to offer your own narrative, one way to tie together and relate those important but disparate measurements.

You have a personal statement.

At most upper-echelon law schools, the personal statement is a two-to-three page document with an open-ended prompt. Some schools provide detailed pointers on what they look for—worth scrutinizing on a school-by-school basis—while others opt for more laconic approaches. In either case, the choice core substance for your essay lies with you. As you begin to brainstorm, keep your audience in mind. It isn't your roommate, it isn't your English professor, and it isn't you yourself. It's a law school admissions officer, one who will read a large batch of similar statements quickly but discerningly. Think of how your essay can tell them something your isolated application parts can't tell, and think of how you can accomplish that in a mere two pages. Think of how you'll stand out—in a good way.

Crafting the statement is a challenge. You've lived a life over two decades in length, and you get only a few paragraphs to condense it all the way down to its essence. The temptation to list accomplishments or experiences is a strong one. Some essays try to pack too much and, as a result, reveal too little about the applicant as a person. Don't struggle to compress a lifetime of experiences into one essay. Instead, think of ways to express who you are through your own voice and a focused selection of illuminating experiences. The specific content of those experiences vary widely from applicant to applicant. You might have a challenge you met and overcame, whether throughout your early life or during the past summer. You might have an encounter that helped you learn and grow. You might have a passion you've followed for years. Whatever you choose, it should speak to who you are—not who your impressive best friend is or what Teach For America does or how much your mother overcame as a child. Ask yourself the question: "What does this say about me?" A good personal statement is just that, a profoundly personal look at the applicant behind the application.

Because the application essay presents such a personal exercise, no single set of steps can guide you through it. This book isn't an instruction manual. It doesn't lay out a precise formula or grand theory for you to follow. You'll find other guides that profess to hand you a comprehensive set of rules and procedures. But if you're pursuing acceptance to a law school, and if you've picked up this book, chances are you don't need a rigid script aimed at the lowest common denominator. Chances are that a cookie-cutter approach will only relegate your essay to the ho-hum middle of a dense, competitive pack. But you can benefit by analyzing, understanding, and internalizing the past's proven routes to success.

55 Successful Harvard Law School Application Essays is composed of a variety of successful essays for you to learn and draw from. On an individual basis, each essay provides just one perspective, but taken as a whole, this book will help you understand how to form an essay both personal and compelling. Every essay in this book secured an author admission to Harvard's top-ranked Law School. While all authors naturally had strong application components beyond the personal statement, we've selected these essays because they represent the sort of superior writing and thinking that contributes to admissions success. The writers and their stories are *sui generis*—so don't worry if you've never founded a tech start-up or battled tsunamis in Samoa—but many of their effective writing techniques and approaches are universal. Don't focus on the particulars of a writer's experiences or feelings and don't measure yourself against them. Focus on how they expressed their experiences effectively and won over the admissions officers who read them.

Each of the fifty-five essays is accompanied by analysis from an editor at *The Harvard Crimson*, Harvard's daily newspaper. The analyses identify strengths as well as weaknesses to help you sift the effective narrative techniques from the ineffective ones. For instance, as you'll see, rote listing of accomplishments and over-long, didactic preaching do not contribute to a positive total effect. Instead, proven, smart strategies include engaging storytelling, concise prose, and thoughtful reflection. Effective essays present a dynamic, realistic image of an author—not as a flat, indefatigable hero, but as a unique individual open to learning and applying that learning to what they are most passionate about.

No essay is perfect, and your first draft especially won't be. But the analyses here will help you apply a critical eye to your own essay that will help you craft a truly compelling and ultimately successful essay that connects with the admissions officers and leads to acceptance at the law school of your choice.

We have sorted the fifty-five personal statements into several broad categories on the basis of content and approach. The seven essay categories we've chosen provide general outlines for the primary types of essays that students write and that have been successful in the past. But the categories are not static. There are essays about world travels that explain personal evolution. There are essays about life's challenges that touch on law school inspiration. There are essays about individual identity that are wound with critical thinking. Your essay may fit one of these categories neatly, or it may stand astride two, three, seven, or even none of them. Whatever the case, it should be an essay that says something important about you and says it clearly and engagingly.

Still, larger themes run throughout that you'll notice as you read. For one, these essays are arguments. They are presentations. They may not resemble your persuasive essays from high school and college (at least, they probably shouldn't), but the arguments, if implicit, remain. The unspoken, underlying thesis is, in its bluntest form, "Accept me." But in more nuanced terms, the essay aims to convey a sense of who you are. And more than that, it should present an argument for who you can and will become. Convey—through experience, thoughtfulness, and voice—that you will make the most of a law school education.

Of course, the precise goals for each essay depend on your personal situation. If your basic information and numbers raise more questions than they answer (such as why you've taken years off from school, or why you're switching careers), the personal statement is the place answer them. If you have a specific vision or a destination motivating your law school application, the personal statement can express that. Above all, ask yourself: "What should my reader know after reading this?" A strong essay will leave an admissions officer feeling that you'll make the most of your potential and that you're committed to growing through your years in law school and beyond. In a related sense, it will leave the reader understanding your mind-set—not every facet, but the ones that count, the ones that set you apart in a good way. On the writing side, a reader should see you clearly and logically articulate your thoughts. An admissions officer shouldn't have to scratch his or her head trying to make sense of a sentence or a paragraph.

After all, the essay and its argument, one of many you'll go on to make in your career, is an exercise in communication. The examples in this book make that clear. As a law school applicant, you undoubtedly have sufficient breadth of experience and ideas to fuel a standout essay, and so do your peers. But pay attention to how these essays articulate their arguments. Notice how they don't merely spit out experiences and ideas but instead process and weave a deliberate mix of past experiences, current situations, and goals for the future. Make sure that the admissions officers get a good idea of who you are and where you intend to go.

But first, take a deep breath. You've already completed the hardest part of the personal statement writing process, and the law school application process as a whole. You've lived as you for years. You've put yourself in a position, after many semesters of study, to apply to a top law school. And you've garnered a wealth of experiences and thoughts. You've already done and thought and lived the topics you'll explore in your personal statement. Wherever you stand in completing the formal application process, you're inches from the finish line in the real one.

So finish strong. The personal statement isn't an obstacle. It's an opportunity. It's a chance to impart a truth about you that your numbers can't fully explain. It's a chance to relate a narrative that integrates application components and your twenty-plus years of life. It's a chance to present *you*—thinking, feeling, analyzing, experiencing, and living. Seize that chance. Start early. Set aside time to read through these sample essays, reflect on your own experiences, and take several more deep breaths. You're almost there. And wherever "there" is for you—a dream job, a career of service, a future with expanded opportunity—you're about to be one step closer.

SECOND EDITION

55
SUCCESSFUL
HARVARD
LAW SCHOOL
APPLICATION
ESSAYS

EVOLUTION

Chances are the "you" of ten, five, or even one year ago looks very different from the person applying to law school today. A full statement about the person you are often requires a look at the changes you have undergone. Essays in this section explain how applicants' mind-sets have been molded and re-molded by experiences and by those around them.

As you trace your own personal evolution, be careful to proceed clearly and avoid covering too much ground. The reader should be able to easily follow your growth and development. Sometimes steps and sequences of events that feel obvious to you, the person who lived them, may seem opaque to an admissions officer.

For some applicants, the tale of evolution demonstrates the vital role of the personal statement in an application. For instance, one writer spent three years toiling in a pharmaceutical company's lab. On its face, the sudden application to law school might seem odd or even suspicious. But his essay paints a broader context of evolution, honing in on the more logical leap from compound creation to chemical patent law. Another writer spent years as a bookstore manager before returning to school, an unconventional path to law school. With context though, his motivation becomes far from early-onset midlife crisis. Instead, his essay weaves a narrative of leadership, parenting, and search for knowledge.

Not everyone needs to explain a unique set of circumstances, but a story of change can take many forms and can highlight a variety of qualities, from openness to discernment to strength tested by adversity. Above all, the story of how you have changed should point to who you are, and to who you see yourself becoming. Every other application component offers a snapshot of who you were or who you are—only the personal statement lets you look to the future.

ANNE-VALERIE PROSPER

"Hi I'm Joleen! I'm from Wisconsin! Where are you from?" trills the pretty brown-eyed girl in my dorm room. I sigh. I would love to have a simple answer to give her and, usually, when confronted with such a daunting question, I smile politely and answer some version of the truth. I try to read her. I wonder if it would be enough to give her the "I'm originally from Haiti" retort. This immediately evokes images of me as a little girl sitting at the kitchen table as my mother cooks "*Grio*" and laughs along to her Maurice Sixto tapes, relishing the Haitian comedian's depiction of Haitian politics. When coming from a country like ours, it's nice to be able to laugh at the folly of it all. This would be an honest answer after all. Although we left Haiti when I was one, my parents enrolled us into a French school in Maryland. We spoke French and Creole at home, I spoke French at school, I ate Haitian food, I listened to Haitian music; we even went back to Haiti twice a year every year—until things got really bad that is. I could always go with a different approach and tell her that I went to high school in Kenya. She might think of me as a world traveler. She might see me as riding *matatus* and playing with orphans, or, she could look at me as some diplomat's child with a driver and uncanny sense of entitlement; unfortunately, back then she would have been right on both accounts.

The thing is, the world attributes who we are with where we are from, and so, for a long time I didn't know who I was. I didn't know where I was from and so I couldn't know where I was going. All of that changed when I got to NYU.

I moved to the big city alone while my parents remained halfway across the world in Nairobi, Kenya. I chose New York because in fourth grade, on a school excursion, I saw *Les Misérables* on Broadway and it changed my life. I moved to New York having lived a very contradictory life. On the one hand, I was quite privileged. The international community in Kenya lived in their own world with their own set of rules. On the other, I had always had a heart for children and had spent much of my time in a baby orphanage known as "The Nest." I looked at these two-week-old infants, children of victims of rape who had died from AIDS and I had a piercing sense that something was not right; we were living in a world of disequilibrium and something had to give. I was going to change the world and I knew that I needed to go to New York; the same place that so beautifully told the story of a French orphan girl.

I had moved around before. I had lived in four places by the time I was eighteen and so I hadn't expected the culture shock to hit me; you always get hit harder when you don't see it coming. The city's stresses slowly but surely took their toll on me. I didn't know what I was doing anymore. Among the actresses and models, away from the slums and the injustice, my big plans didn't seem so feasible anymore. It wasn't until the second semester of college, when I joined a Christian fellowship on campus that my vision came back to life. I came to Christ that year and, later, with tentative support from my parents I moved into a house in the Bronx and became one third of the nonprofit organization A House on Beekman. We felt the biblical call to serve the poor and for us New Yorkers, Beekman Avenue was where we could do that. It was a far cry from the Kibera slums but it was the land of single teenage mothers who were victims of domestic violence. It was the place where dozens of kids had absentee parents and appreciated a healthy snack and a good story. These people weren't as poor as the people in Kenya, but they were marginalized. I started to see the other forms of oppression that existed. My roommates and I began to share all of our clothes and as we grew in community, God grew our ministry. More kids started showing up for family dinner on Monday night. More "gang members" started calling us "Ma'am" and pulling their pants up as they walked into our home. Living here has shown me what it is to serve in the United States. God continued to grow my intolerance for injustice when I received an internship at an immigration law firm. We mostly worked with asylum cases and as I walked into the conference room wearing a suit, and sat across a girl my age who was being forced to be the fourth wife of a seventy-five-year-old or who had to undergo female genital mutilation to be eligible for marriage, day after day after day, something in me snapped. I decided I was going to law school. I decided that I couldn't live a life that glossed over the gravest injustices of the world. I realized that I could hold orphans for months or give our Bronx kids healthy snacks for weeks, but that one day, I was going to die. One day, my roommates will die as will the lawyers at the law firm that I work at. I need to be a part of systematic change. I need to be a part of something bigger than the one life I have been given. I knew I was graduating in December, and so I applied to the International Justice Mission. I will be working there as the Human Rights intern in D.C. from January through April. My projects will be in Haiti, Ecuador, and Peru. I finally get to partner with lawyers who are changing the system from the inside out.

Through all of these experiences I finally realized where I was from. I realized that I am a child of God and a citizen of the world and this has led me to where I am going. I am going to law school. I am going to get a degree that allows my voice to be loud enough for all us world citizens. I am going to be part of the redemption that far outlasts the one small life that I have lived.

Analysis

Admissions officers certainly see many tropes repeated in application essay after application essay. There's the "overcoming adversity" story. There's the "look at my passion" narrative. There's the "I have finally discovered myself" reflection. Without a doubt, these archetypes can get stale, especially for someone who is reading them as part of their full-time job. The power of this essay arises from its masterful ability to synthesize those well-worn application genres into a compelling story of personal growth. One of the hallmarks of a successful application essay is the ability to capture the reader's attention—to draw him or her out of the monotony of reading prosaic bullet points that do little more than list the achievements that already appear on applicants' résumés.

While Anne-Valerie Prosper does not skimp on her personal accomplishments or her coming-of-age story, she takes those tropes and successfully brings them to life. Rather than account important aspects of her life, she grapples with them vividly, giving the reader a privileged look at both the details of her life and the lucidity of her mind.

Although Prosper does a formidable job integrating the various elements of her identity and development, she occasionally overextends herself. For instance, the reference to *Les Misérables* is accompanied by minimal interpretation or explanation. And the attribution "it changed my life" sounds odd and exaggerated, especially beside the compelling, real-world examples she provides. Of course, viewing the play might truly have been transformative, but unless the reader can understand and appreciate that influence, a reference like Prosper's can cause more trouble than it is worth.

Nonetheless, after reading this essay, the reader gains unique insight into who this author is and what makes her tick. She isn't as she lays out the case for herself, but she does impart a meaningful message all the same. There it is, right in the essay—impossible to pinpoint but also impossible to ignore.

—John F. M. Kocsis

ERIC T. ROMEO

Eighteen months ago, I viewed my career path as very divergent from that of my parents; both were attorneys, and I was a scientist. I had just entered my third year of employment at a major pharmaceutical company, and I was starting to come into my own as a medicinal chemist and making significant impacts on our drug discovery programs. I was working side by side with incredibly talented people at the cutting edge of my field, and yet I felt strangely unfulfilled. I began to reassess my plans for doctoral study in chemistry and in doing so, reflected on my path thus far.

My scientific career began in earnest in the chemistry lab of Professor William Armstrong at Boston College. Due to a lack of funding and resources at that time, I was given full reign over a research project normally reserved for graduate students. To compound the challenge, the research was centered in bioinorganic chemistry, something I had never studied before. Nevertheless, the prospect of leaving behind my textbooks and designing my own experiments proved sufficient motivation for me to start finding my way. With the generous support of my faculty adviser and labmates, my research grew over the next year and a half to include two other undergraduates, and produced an award-winning thesis project. The collaboration and problem-solving skills I learned in the Armstrong Lab would become invaluable as I moved into the next phase of my career, the pharmaceutical industry.

When I arrived at Merck Research Labs in the summer of 2007, I was excited to finally put to use the teachings from my favorite college class, synthetic organic chemistry. Unfortunately, I quickly learned that doing chemistry on paper is very different from doing it in real life. Because associate chemists at Merck are expected to spend most of their time making compounds in the lab, my lack of experience with organic chemistry techniques meant that I would have to start from scratch if I were to succeed. Thankfully, my experience of being thrown into the deep end at school prepared me well for this dousing, and with the help and patience of my manager, my skills in the lab grew by the day. Eventually, I became comfortable enough making compounds that I was able to think about designing and optimizing them. Delving into the patent literature and finding free intellectual property space to make novel drug candidates became my favorite task at work, and before long I was named as a coinventor on my first of five U.S. Patent Applications. It slowly became apparent that what I really liked about my job was not the chemistry of drug design, but the problem solving and strategy involved. I found myself in a quandary: I had fallen in love with the process of doing science, not just science itself.

The remedy for my dilemma was provided in short order by a "Patent Law 101" presentation given by members of our in-house counsel. There, I was introduced to the idea that intellectual property, rather than internal research and development, is the true life-blood of the pharmaceutical industry. It quickly became clear to me that the ability to create, protect, and manage this resource effectively is essential to generating the necessary revenue to fund all of a drug company's other functions, including my chemistry department. As the session drew to a close, I realized that intellectual property law, in the context of pharmaceuticals, offered me an opportunity to combine my aptitude for drug discovery with my love of creative problem solving. Over the next year, I met with patent attorneys both within and outside of the pharmaceutical industry to discuss my path forward. Additionally, I was able to attend a patent trial in Federal Court, and found the challenge of explaining science to the lay jury fascinating. In sum, these experiences served to further crystallize my desire to enter the field of law.

I intend to pursue a career in intellectual property law with a focus on chemistry and drug discovery. Therein, I hope to leverage my skills and experience as a medicinal chemist to provide clients with the unique perspective of someone who has stood in their shoes. I believe that such enhanced communication and understanding would foster a more collaborative, innovative, and productive discovery environment. I am confident that my past experiences in solving new and difficult problems will facilitate my ability to discover the common ground between the rule of law and the laws of science.

Analysis

Every good essay makes a point to emphasize the positive qualities of the applicant. This one certainly takes home the trophy, punching out a different theme at the end of each anecdote. The first paragraph ends with an assertion of Eric Romeo's self-reflection and evaluation skills. The second brings out his quick adaptability and independent learning abilities. The third showcases his creativity in producing chemical compounds and willingness to seize and make the most of opportunities given to him. The fourth tells of his enthusiasm for his newfound passion, and his impeccable motivation and drive in pursuing his interests. Each paragraph homes in on a specific trait, and each fits with the others like the pieces of a puzzle that compose and present the ideal applicant.

Still, this essay does take on a fairly daunting task—explaining a career switch—and that comes with its pitfalls. Romeo sets the stage for his switch with the line, "I had fallen in love with the process of doing science, not just science itself." That line raises more questions than answers: Isn't a job in science a fusion of those aspects? Romeo then leaps to a presentation, and in a flash he is a law school applicant. The shift is abrupt. He doesn't need to attribute the shift to a single moment or quandary. The essay is at its best when it tracks his organic interest in patent law and its yearlong evolution.

That said, Romeo appeals to the applicative nature of careers in law by emphasizing his underlying passion for drug discovery, which drives his interest in intellectual property law. He ties this together in the last paragraph, where he specifically states how his indispensable previous experience in organic chemistry will assist him in his law studies, and how it grants him a unique perspective as a law practitioner.

—*Luke Chang*

ZAIN JINNAH

My university experience tore apart the foundations of everything I believed in.

Three years ago, I entered university with high ambitions but no target. I aimed to work hard, complete my degree in three years instead of four, and then study law to earn my way to a prestigious political career. I had a powerful passion for politics and was quite certain of my political views. I was also quite religious, and held a high degree of certainty in the veracity of my faith. These two elements formed the core of who I was at the time, but my first year of university would completely dismantle these convictions. In their place, it would instill a sense of confusion that persists to this day.

Curious about the new intellectual environment I had entered, I ventured to learn more about the faith of others by engaging in interfaith initiatives. But increased contact with those from within my own religious community bewildered me, as I encountered different perspectives that I found difficult to reconcile with my own. Looking outward to other religious traditions only confounded me further. Concurrently, my courses in political science shattered the positive conception I had of world politics and left in its place a dismal portrait of an international system motivated by power and greed. With my fundamental beliefs broken apart, I delved into the academic study of both of these areas in search of definitive answers. The lack thereof only led me into deeper confusion, and I wandered about in search of something certain to grab onto.

My second semester brought me to a world politics course that exposed me to the tragic human consequences of the twenty-first century's major wars. I became livid about the political calculations made at the expense of human rights, and set off on a path of actively opposing such actions. Learning about the injustices imposed on the world's marginalized really hit home for me, for as the son of two parents who had been made refugees by one such situation I had seen firsthand the implications they had on the lives of the affected. My identities as an Indian and a Muslim, as well as my African heritage, heightened my personal attachment to the sense of injustice that began to overwhelm me.

Gradually, a sense of direction emerged from my frustration at the state of the world. My anger at the precedence of politics over human rights was supplanted by a desire to better comprehend the globe's political system so that I could effect change within it. As I delved deeper into the world of international affairs—reading books and watching documentaries for hours each day, engaging in deep conversation with acquaintances of diverse backgrounds so as to better understand the issues that affect their countries—an overarching purpose emerged: justice. I wanted to devote all my efforts to the pursuit of justice for those without the means to defend themselves. The consistent outrage I felt upon learning of the adversities imposed on others solidified my resolve to contribute to a more equitable political system.

Yet my confusion over both religion and politics continued. My quest for the correct political disposition had taken me to the left and the right of the spectrum to no avail, while my religious journey had left me more lost than ever. But something had changed. Now, I found certainty in my confusion. My search brought me to explore many different religious traditions, and though the differences among them didn't help to resolve my uncertainty I found that a common vein ran through each of their philosophies. The same common vein that transcended political ideology and was present in every political perspective, liberal or conservative, that I examined. Justice. It didn't just exist in the realms of politics and human rights, but was an omnipresent idea. I realized that despite the myriad of factors that differentiate people, every human being and every philosophy aspires to justice, whatever it perceives that term to mean. I discovered that justice is universal, and it was this realization that helped me to find my way again. Despite still being quite lost, I had found a guiding light.

Three years on, that light has provided my life with purpose, direction, and cohesion. Everything about me—my worldview, my interactions with those around me, my ambitions for the future—revolves around that central concept. Nearly ten years of leadership in student activism, over six hundred hours of volunteering in my community, and an extremely successful academic career fueled by my newfound passion have cemented my certainty that I am on the right path. Faithfully, I follow my conscience as it directs me to dedicate myself to others rather than simply enriching myself. This light has given me a new foundation, and I want to build upon that foundation with an education in the most just of disciplines. I believe that Harvard, as an institution known for producing leaders who have changed the world for the better, is the ideal venue for such an education. With its unparalleled opportunities in international and human rights law, Harvard Law will provide me with the skills and intellectual conditioning necessary to make a meaningful contribution toward justice in the international system.

Analysis

The structure of this essay is very logical. Zain Jinnah describes the intellectual confusion of his university years and through clear and strongly worded prose, leads the reader through his mental transformation as he comes to terms with the world's inconsistencies. His motivation for applying to law school—a desire to pursue justice on behalf of the marginalized—feels somewhat overdone, and yet thanks to a step-by-step narrative that describes the exact thought process through which he realized the importance of justice, the cliché is tempered and his interest feels more natural.

Indeed, Jinnah threads the salient details about his own history into the essay very well; instead of stating his background in a block at the beginning, he specifically includes his parents' refugee status and cultural heritage to clarify why the broader narrative is personally important. By establishing a context for his change and growth, this makes the essay much more convincing.

Less convincing is Jinnah's tendency at times to slip into melodrama. He waxes poetic about his shift from search to revelation. The themes of a new "guiding light" and absolute statements, like everything now "revolves around that central concept," oversell a meaningful transition. Instead, he might have focused more on the substance of that transition and of the response to injustice he identifies. Rather than pay lip service to his own identity, he might have expounded on his personal response to injustice. Furthermore, Jinnah doesn't have all the answers yet—that's why he's applying to law school—and he doesn't need to make it seem that way.

On that note, Jinnah's statement is refreshing when it does embrace uncertainty, a sign that he understands the complexity of intellectual pursuit but has persevered as an academic nonetheless.

This spirit is welcome at the graduate school level because it indicates awareness that scholarship, while necessary to make the world a better place, is not always easy. It is important, however, that Jinnah clearly identifies the objectives that such realizations have prompted; this suggests that he is goal-driven, a problem-solver, and determined—all critical qualities for a lawyer. That he does not state these traits outright but instead lets them appear through a well-crafted anecdote, is appropriately subtle.

Overall, this essay is strong because it is easy to follow and well written and identifies a passionate reason for joining the field of law. Jinnah isn't done growing and has a long way left to attain his goals, but the reader is left with an important, enduring impression. Jinnah has the energy and commitment to keep going.

—Radhika Jain

JIMMIE STRONG

Police sirens drew near. The sound of a fire truck followed. Then, an ambulance appeared. The scene that led to the arrival of these vehicles forced me into maturity. First, I heard my stepfather, Brody, lecturing Mom. Shortly thereafter, I heard Mom scream. I was only ten, but I ran downstairs to help. Brody was choking Mom and ramming her head into the wall. I squealed, "Get your hands off Mom!" While his focus shifted, Mom dialed some numbers and hung up. Our phone rang, but Brody's sermon—nonviolently resumed to avoid my wrath—had our attention; but unlike on Sundays, a police siren silenced him. Mom rushed to the door and shouted, "Arrest him! Arrest him! He hit me!" Mom had dialed 9-1-1, hung up, and purposely ignored callbacks; this signaled the operator to send emergency vehicles.

The next day, I spoke to the school's guidance counselor. She said that I could be open and honest with her, but I calmly said, "I'm fine." Witnessing domestic violence only watered seeds of intellectual maturity that had been planted by events in my early childhood. At age two, I recall accompanying my father to the residence of the woman who later gave birth to my younger brother, playing with her children, and telling Mom about my experiences. I remember my parents getting divorced, my mom struggling to build a new life, and my grandparents taking me in. Way before I saw domestic violence, I knew—as Achebe says—that "Things Fall Apart." Understanding that things fall apart wasn't comforting in itself, but I was able to say, "I'm fine," because I knew that things—however bad they seemed—could be put back together.

A calm, "I'm fine," was the result of having seen my family rally to put things back together after my parents' divorce. Mom moved from the home she shared with my father in Jackson, Mississippi, to my aunt's house in Memphis, Tennessee. While Mom worked two jobs so she could afford an apartment in a good school district, my grandparents took me into their home in Duncan, Mississippi, and prepared me for school and life. Grandma taught me everything from respectful manners to reading. Granddad showed me how to work hard; regardless of rain, heat, or cold, Granddad and I worked our land. Working land of his own was Granddad's dream; he and Grandma, however, purposely sent me to Memphis with a different dream. Daily Grandma asked, "L'il Jim, you gon' be a doctor or a lawyer?" I always chose lawyer, and Granddad always said, "It's gon' be hard, but you can do it."

Though I thought Granddad's words were about educational rigor, witnessing domestic violence showed me that he was referring to unexpected obstacles that can derail one's dream. Thanks to a wealth of wisdom, my dream never faded; and during senior year of high school, my childhood dream became a conscious career decision. Through Tennessee's Youth in Government program, I argued a case on Miranda Rights in Tennessee's Supreme Court. The entire process—from combing case law to briefing and presenting the case—proved so exhilarating that I closed the case on considering other careers. With regard to choosing an area of legal expertise, the jury was still out. In fact, one of my favorite aspects of law was its ability to add value to all arenas, from Corporate America to the nonprofit sector.

My career aspirations gained specificity during my second year of college on my first trip outside the United States. While studying abroad in Rome, Italy, I tackled my first business classes: upper-level courses in business and marketing and a course on economic and political structures of the European Union. Challenging coursework—assignments that made me use all my previous experiences and explore unfamiliar phenomena—shaped my legal aspirations. My international business course, for example, forced me to use my limited stock of legal expertise, business savvy, and political acumen to explain how I would've minimized Enron's mistakes in India. While on a mental voyage to India's Maharashtra state, I phoned to Houston and advised Kenneth Lay not to be swayed by the Congress Party's promises of economic reform, as the power to control laws regulating business practices was shifting to parties that opposed promised reforms. Unique challenges like this confronted me every day, and I loved that.

Upon completing my program, I realized that the experiences that molded my strengths—seven years of studying international relations, six years of running my own business, and one career-defining semester of legal training—could all be used in one area of the legal field, international business law. Through Sidley Austin

LLP's Prelaw Scholars Initiative, I conversed with international business attorneys and learned how to best prepare myself for my legal career. Harvard's Law and Business program provides the international transactional, litigation, and regulatory expertise that I need to excel in my career. I can imagine nothing better than returning to Duncan, Mississippi—where Google searches for black lawyers yield no names—and showing children that they can be attorneys from Harvard Law.

Analysis

In Jimmie Strong's essay, Strong describes how his childhood experiences—particularly, witnessing domestic violence—influenced his maturity and inspired him to become a lawyer and how this childhood dream was shaped by his academic experiences later in life. How Strong's essay transitions from one subject to another fluidly and provides strong examples of his intellectual and emotional fortitude make the essay a particularly compelling read.

Strong's essay begins with a suspenseful description of a domestic violence incident between his stepfather and his mother. Strong explains the purpose of this anecdote without compromising the suspense by stating, "The scene that led to the arrival of these [emergency] vehicles forced me into maturity," although he may overplay the extent to which that experience—and not the hardship that preceded it—drove his maturing. Though the content matter is extremely sensitive, Strong provides just enough detail to understand the story without distracting from a sense of its influence on his development. From the retelling of this night, he transitions to how watching his family recover from divorce and domestic violence gave him a strong sense of perseverance.

Strong then transitions from his childhood to his senior year of high school when he participated in Tennessee's Youth in Government program. He sneaks in a few clever legal puns when describing how he "closed the case" on other professions after this experience. The following paragraph focuses on his experiences with the law in his undergraduate education but it is important to note that even though Strong's essay follows a chronological structure, it describes his evolving relationship with the law and how his interests become more precise.

The essay loses some of its focus and strength as it nears the end. Ticking off various experiences and achievements feels like a forced afterthought following the concise and powerful body of the essay. The personal statement is only one aspect of an application, and the points Strong tacks on in closing should show up in other components. Strong could have left the reader with a more lasting image and feeling if he concluded closer to thoughts in the line that ends, "from Corporate America to the nonprofit sector."

The last sentence—which states that he would like nothing better than returning to his hometown to serve as a role model for young children as a Harvard attorney—feels oddly sentimental and unexpected since he did not mention this intent previously in the essay, but it nonetheless makes an adequate end to an artful and persuasive essay.

—Hayley Cuccinello

BRIAN AUNE

At the time, I wasn't sure of my answer: "I think a good manager knows he or she doesn't have all the answers, but does know where to look for them." I was twenty-three and applying for a position many people didn't think I was ready for. I felt small. The question was, "What do you think makes a good manager?" Almost seven years later, I have learned from experience that leadership is all about finding answers to difficult questions. I have worked hard to develop this ability, and now I am seeking to use it at a higher level. I see law school as the chance to make that happen.

I have been gainfully employed since I was fourteen and spent over ten years in leadership positions. Six of those years were spent managing a branch of a major national bookstore that had fifty employees and annual sales of $8 million. But those statistics don't really tell you what I did. I answered questions. Questions such as: "Where can we find another fifteen thousand dollars in sales by tomorrow?" "Can I hire two new employees for the café?" "How can we get this employee to do his job better?" Some of my most fulfilling moments were walking through the store with a line of employees forming behind me, discussing each person's questions and finding answers together. We've all had managers we listened to because we were required to, and ones we listened to because we were inspired to. When people responded to me as they did at the bookstore, it gave me hope that, at least occasionally, I was in the latter category. I look at the store now and find gratification at seeing employees I hired serving as effective leaders, and policies and procedures I established continuing to serve a new management team.

During this time I also had the great pleasure of being a stepfather. For ten years, I helped raise a little girl from the age of seven. She was an incredibly accepting stepdaughter, but let me just say, if there are lessons in patience you do not learn as a manager, you will learn them as a parent. At the bookstore my contribution was important, but it was mainly limited to that store, or at most, that company. As a parent, I helped shape how another person experienced the world. Here, I didn't just help her make decisions. I tried to teach her how to find the answers on her own. You raise this child and attempt to give her all the tools to prepare her for a life you cannot predict. Hopefully, if you did enough things right and not too many things wrong, her life will be limited only by her own desires and not her parents' vision.

Since that time, aided by several personal and professional changes, I decided to seek out a career in which I could apply my growing leadership skills toward a larger goal. That is what led me to give up my management position and return to school. The time I had spent in management led to a seven-year hiatus between starting and finishing my undergraduate degree. While that break may make me older and less fun than my peers, it has also given me a maturity that has served me well in my return to the university. Unlike many undergraduates, I know why I'm in school and I want to be here. I returned to school to find a forum in which I could use the leadership skills I have been developing toward a greater purpose, but I consciously did not limit my perception of what that forum might look like. I studied communication as a potential tool to effect change, and political science to be exposed to social issues that may need changing.

It was in a law and religion class that I found greater focus. This class examined first amendment cases involving such issues as school prayer, state voucher use for private religious schools, and religious practice rights. In reading these cases, I identified with the legal process behind the decisions. It may be idealistic, but I began to see the law as a means of seeking social justice using analysis and reason rather than strategy and emotion, and this felt familiar to me. I saw a parallel between the legal reasoning process and what I had done as a manager for so many years. I have heard it described that constitutional law is the reverse of regulatory law. While regulatory law is written by the government to dictate what the people can and cannot do, constitutional law is written by the people to regulate what the government can and cannot do. I want to play a role in the formation of decisions regarding social justice issues. Working in constitutional law would allow me to apply the skills I developed as a leader toward this goal. Just as when I was a manager, my role would be to understand the legal questions and relevant policies, and work with others to find the best answers.

At this early stage, I am drawn to the more intellectual pursuits of the law. I see myself potentially working as an appellate attorney or perhaps someday as a professor. However, as with my undergraduate schooling, I do not enter this with a specific idea of what I will do, for too specific a goal could narrow my latitude of exposure. I want to attend law school for the education, not the degree. As I study and work in the law I hope to find myself back in a familiar place—where I don't know all the answers, but I do know where to look.

Analysis

This candidate's introduction is strong. Its message is thoughtful, one that frames the rest of the essay nicely. In the first paragraph, Brian Aune explains what leadership means to him; in the second, he demonstrates, convincingly, that it's a quality that he possesses. More impressively, he gives the admissions officer the impression that he is not only goal-oriented and strategic, but also human and relatable.

Aune uses concrete examples from his professional life to make his point, and he makes his point well. In general, it could be risky to take this approach: Writing too much about work can make the essay feel like a rehashing of the résumé (which will likely also be boring to read). Aune avoids this pitfall by meaningfully adding substance, giving texture to the title "bookstore manager."

Though personal anecdotes can certainly add color, the paragraph about the candidate's stepdaughter seems unnecessary. Were it to convey something about his character or personality or hiatus from school, it would have been fine to include. In this essay, it doesn't add much and distracts quite a bit. In the next paragraph, Aune does provide information that aids in painting a clear picture of him as a law school applicant: He explains his reasoning for returning to school after a seven-year hiatus. Given that this question is probably on the admissions officer's mind, it's a smart one to devote space to.

The next section of the essay is weaker. An important task for the applicant in the personal statement is to convey why he/she is pursuing a law degree. His points about religion, social justice, and wanting to use the legal system to *apply* his leadership skills could be very effective—both in proving his passion for the law and in tying the essay together—had they been elaborated on and clarified. On the whole, a more focused essay would have made a more compelling essay. His ultimate challenge is to explain his ostensibly abrupt motivation for attending law school. Perhaps most troublesome is Aune's failure to explain what he will do after law school—he openly admits that he isn't sure what he will do as an attorney, which can be problematic with such a talented applicant pool.

The essay would have been much stronger had Aune given specific reasons for his interest in becoming a lawyer. But throughout his personal statement, he shows that he's likable, effective, and likely to be successful in whatever pursuit he eventually chooses.

—*Lisa Mogilanski*

MICHELE GAUGER

If I were to write a book about my life up to this point, I would en-
title it *Stories of an Ivory Tower Refugee*. I often think of myself as a
refugee, escaping a future in biological research not meant for me.

During the first three years of graduate school, I planned to finish my dissertation, go on to a postdoctoral fellowship in biological
research, and then apply for a faculty position at a university. This
progression of events is instilled in graduate students as being the
most noble and distinguished path, and deviation from this path is
often viewed by the academic community as compromising one's
scientific integrity. This notion that there was a prescribed course
graduate students were expected to follow after obtaining their
degrees was always very frustrating to me. I decided to pursue an
advanced degree to open doors for my career, but rather, I felt that
I was being encouraged to follow a predetermined course. Stub-
bornly, I went along with this plan even in the face of signs that it
was not the right choice for me. It was not until midway through
my fourth year of graduate school that I began to seriously consider an alternative career.

Since the fourth year of dissertation work is generally regarded
as the most angst-ridden, I thought that perhaps my wavering career
aspirations were merely a result of my frustration with lab research.
However, as time went on, my desire to find a career path that I
would enjoy won out over my stubbornness, and I finally accepted
the conclusion I had been trying so hard to avoid—my future did
not lie in scientific research.

Although deciding to change career paths meant acknowledging
that I had been wrong about my career aspirations for the past eight
years, once I made my decision I felt a tremendous sense of peace.
I began to really look forward to my future, knowing that I had
made the right decision.

It is my desire to pursue a career in patent law, which greatly informs my decision to attend law school. A career in patent law will
allow me to apply my scientific knowledge in a new field while not
altogether abandoning science. I became interested in patent law

after discussing career possibilities with an acquaintance currently working at a small patent firm. Like me, she had pursued and obtained her doctorate in science. After becoming dissatisfied with her work as a postdoctoral fellow, she became a successful patent attorney. I had the opportunity to consult with her on a few projects and became more familiar with some of the duties of a patent attorney, such as patent application drafting and communicating with biotechnology company management. While I am eager to acquire a wealth of practical knowledge of many areas of law, I am particularly excited that a career as a patent attorney will allow me to utilize both my background in scientific research and science degree.

Throughout college, I hoped to eventually spend my days walking around in a lab coat and goggles. Today, that is precisely what I'm doing as a biochemistry graduate student. But plans can change, and being open to changing one's plan is crucial to recognizing one's full potential. Many people have asked me why, after six years of graduate school, I would want to undergo another three years of education when I could get a job with the degree I have now. My answer is always the same—yes, I could get a job, maybe even one I'd like. But by changing my plan, I'll have the opportunity to discover a career in which I can fully recognize my own potential and not only like my job, but love it.

Analysis

Why would a Harvard Law School applicant call herself an "Ivory Tower Refugee"? By doing so, Michele Gauger strategically transforms a common problem for law school applicants—an unconventional past—into a strength.

In her statement, Gauger solves a tricky résumé riddle: eight years devoted to a career in biological research and not law. She wisely frames her path from lab to law school as a narrative. Stories are compelling, and in the process of detailing her own, Gauger anticipates and addresses many questions an admissions officer would have. For example, she explains her single-minded focus on science (and presumably, not law) by describing the rigid expectations of scientific graduate school. Gauger demonstrates her humility by revealing personal weaknesses, such as stubbornness, that kept her imprisoned in the ivory tower.

Next, Gauger includes a key component of all good stories, and personal statements: a turning point. She shows that by changing career paths, she has overcome her weaknesses and become more flexible, ready to pursue her true passion—law. (However, Gauger might do well to explain a bit more thoroughly why biological research was the wrong path for her.)

And her precise leap from scientist to law school applicant could also use more specificity, though—a stumbling block for many essays looking to explain a similar shift. She reduces a complex evolution to a conversation with a single friend. It's doubtful that one conversation made all the difference. It's also likely that expounding on that subtle, complex evolution would make for a stronger essay, and make her a stronger applicant.

But Gauger does well to home in on a specific branch of law, patent, that interests her and that would draw upon her scientific background. The end of the essay reinforces the overall pitch to admissions officers: that Gauger's decision to abandon a scientific career is not a foolhardy whim, but her greatest asset as a law school candidate.

—*Julia F. P. Ostmann*

SUZANNE TURNER

It is my belief that a person should contribute positively to their community and their society, and the practice of law has been a natural choice for me. As far back as I can remember I have wanted to pursue a career as a local prosecutor, and came to law school with that career path in mind. My experience this summer as the legal intern to the Appeals Division of the Essex County District Attorney's office has confirmed my commitment to this path. Furthermore, I have long contributed to public interest work, focusing my efforts particularly in the areas of social justice and civil rights.

During my first year at the George Washington University Law School, I worked hard to develop my legal writing skills and was recently selected as a Writing Fellow for the 2009 to 2010 school year. If accepted to Harvard Law School, I look forward to pursuing similar academic opportunities that would enable me to contribute to the law school community. I bring a well-rounded perspective to that community, having worked as a paralegal both in the high-stakes world of corporate litigation and for a small, local plaintiff's bar firm before beginning my legal studies.

My leadership positions with George Washington Law's American Civil Liberties Union and Law Students for Reproductive Justice student groups complements the work ethic and organizational skills I developed during my three years of work experience. At the close of the school year, I was elected copresident of both organizations. The opportunities presented by my involvement, particularly interacting with practitioners in various fields, were vital to my goal of achieving a well-rounded legal education. I was also a member of the Street Law program, participating both as a teacher in seventh- and eighth-grade classrooms and by writing lesson plans in the areas of constitutional and criminal law.

Although I was new to the District of Columbia last year, I also became an active participant in local public interest organizations. My most significant role has been with the National Capital Area ACLU's Future Leaders Council, a coalition of student leaders from the ACLU's high school, undergraduate, and law school clubs.

I was recently elected as the Vice Chair of the council. I also participated in a joint ACLU-American Constitution Society initiative in September where volunteers taught lessons in constitutional law to eighth graders in public schools around the city. I have greatly enjoyed working in my local community, particularly in ways that may encourage urban youth to realize and explore the diverse possibilities of a legal education.

While living and working in New York City from 2005 to 2007, I volunteered with several public interest groups: the New York City Alliance Against Sexual Assault, the New York Civil Liberties Union, Planned Parenthood Federation of America, and the Human Rights Campaign. I mainly participated in grassroots initiatives, and was a volunteer for the Human Rights Campaign's annual gala.

I have thoroughly enjoyed my experience at GW Law, but have decided to settle in the Boston area. Transferring to Harvard Law School would allow me to expend my academic and volunteer efforts in the community where I intend to live and work. I am drawn to Harvard Law because of its reputation for excellence. I am particularly attracted to your Criminal Prosecution Perspectives clinic providing the opportunity to act as a student prosecutor in the District Courts. I would also look forward to exploring the Family, Domestic Violence and LGBT Law clinic, as I have long been devoted to issues of LGBT rights and family policy.

I realize that my undergraduate academic accomplishments at Cornell were less than outstanding, and may not be typical of your admitted students. My undergraduate focus was largely on my military training until an injury required discharge. My aptitude is better illustrated by my recent successes in law school. I worked exceptionally hard at George Washington this past year, earning above a 4.0 grade point average for the spring semester. I have been designated a George Washington Scholar, indicating a cumulative GPA within the top 1 to 15 percent of my class. I also devoted a great deal of time to extracurricular activities at the law school and in the community. I will bring that same level of dedication, work ethic, and passion for public interest law to the remainder of my legal education and beyond, and would welcome the increased challenge of the Harvard Law School curriculum. Thank you for any consideration you are able to give my application.

Analysis

Suzanne Turner's personal statement extensively shows her credentials and assets that make her a qualified candidate. An aspect that stands out in her essay is that she states her strengths (such as her comprehensive legal writing skills), and supports these claims with the work that she has done (being a Writing Fellow at George Washington University Law School). It is advantageous to have law schools know of her qualifications and how she will be an asset to the school with her strengths. She successfully did this many times throughout her essay while indicating that she has a well-rounded legal education. Moreover, Turner makes clear what field within law that she is interested in pursuing, particularly in relation to the program at the Harvard Law School. This shows why Turner is interested in pursuing not just law school, but law school particularly at Harvard. Although it is not necessarily required to state exactly what one plans on pursuing, it is only beneficial to do so for it indicates that the candidate has a clear goal in mind and will aspire toward it.

In this essay, however, Turner falls into listing too many qualifications, credentials, and accomplishments. These are already listed on her résumé, so the essay was her chance to show her personality and maybe use a small set of accomplishments or experiences as a framework to support her argument. Remember the question: What should my reader know after reading this? In this case, it may not amount to much more than the rest of the application manages. A stronger strategy would have given the reader an understanding of who Suzanne Turner is in light of her experiences. By not interpreting her experiences beyond the platitudinous "I have greatly enjoyed," and "I have thoroughly enjoyed," Turner misses out on an opportunity to fully leverage the personal statement.

That said, Turner's case is unique. For one, she is a transfer student. With that comes a strong burden to explain her situation and her switch. Most of the accomplishments she rather stiffly lists are related to her tenure at George Washington Law School, and that emphasis of work and progress she has made since first applying to law school helps bolster her transfer case. Turner also touches on how Harvard Law offers opportunities she cannot access now. Turner could certainly do a better job processing experiences like her summer internship, but in her case, breadth of accomplishment matters as much as depth.

Near the essay's close, Turner tackles the issue of a subpar undergraduate transcript head-on. She first explains the poor GPA as a product of her military commitment. And then she shows how her results have changed along with her circumstances. The line, "My aptitude is better illustrated by my recent successes in law school," comports well with her overall message of recent success, and deftly frames that success as the true lens for observing her potential. Turner takes advantage of her application's one chance to explain, in her own words, the unique case she presents, and it goes a long way for her.

—*Mariam H. Jalloul*

TELLING A STORY

You don't need to chronicle your entire life in a personal statement. The connections among you, law school, and your topic of choice might not even be obvious. A simple, well-told vignette can still speak volumes about you as a person and as a prospective lawyer. The stories range from a few hours in length to broader looks at the development of a skill or other effort. Essays in this category recount stories from applicants' lives, often with a literary flair that also serves to demonstrate an aptitude for the written word.

In recounting an anecdote, remember that your ultimate goal is to make a case for yourself as a law school applicant. You shouldn't be making a case for your friend who stars in an interesting story. And you shouldn't be making a case for your adroitness with ornate prose or punchy dialogue. First make sure the content reflects the message you aim to send. Then make sure your writing communicates it.

Ensuring that readers understand the meaning behind your story can prove tricky, too. Your audience isn't a classroom of English students conducting meticulous literary analysis; it's an admissions officer perusing a thick stack of essays. You shouldn't dumb down your ideas or rely on phrasing like "this example shows that . . ." or "as this story demonstrates . . ." but your message should be clear and relatable. If it is, your story, even a brief glimpse spanning a few hours, will say a lot about who you are as a writer, thinker, and person.

JACQUELINE YUE

Like any turning point in life, senior year involves soul-searching, and I have spent many evenings reflecting on my memories at Penn. Inevitably, my mind turns to Mary.

After we first met during our dorm's welcome-to-college barbecue party, coincidences ensured that Mary and I would continue running into each other. Since we were both early risers, we met for breakfast every day. Our classes were in the same buildings because we both adored the humanities. We even shared extracurricular interests—three or four evenings a week, we walked together to the gym for waltz and tango lessons. It did not take long for us to become close friends, and prior to leaving for spring break, we submitted forms to be roommates.

That was never to be. Although Mary had seemed fine one week ago, when I saw her again, she walked with a limp and spoke haltingly. I spent the next three hours with her at student health services, forgetting that I still had morning classes. It was not until she was sent to the emergency room that I finally left, promising to find her if she had to stay overnight. I had no idea then that my first visit that evening would be followed by so many others.

Mary never left the hospital, and the lessons I learned in the next few months are among the most significant I have had in my life. I became more attentive. Noticing the marginally edible hospital fare, I asked a doctor about nutrition and began toting over meals for both of us. I brought and peeled oranges for her after I saw her eyes light up when she first spied one among her breakfast items. By recalling allusions to tests and papers, I mentally pieced together her schedule and went to her classes, first to collect her homework, then to ask for extensions on everything. And as it became increasingly difficult for Mary to talk, I learned to read her face. Gradually, I overcame my shyness as I approached doctors for what they would disclose about my friend's health. I asked Mary's classmates to visit her, and when her parents arrived from

Note: To respect my friend's privacy, I have used a different name.

Beijing, I forgot my insecurity over my Chinese and tried my best to comfort them.

I became more compassionate. Whereas I would formerly have balked at the idea of spending time with a friend on the eve of a test, my linguistics midterm was the last thing on my mind as I sat by Mary's bedside and held her hand until she fell asleep. I ran from the hospital at one end of the campus to our dorm at the other up to three times a night to bring her things she had forgotten. And whenever Mary grew angry at me over something, I blushed and apologized. If having someone to blame made her illness more bearable, then that was all that mattered.

When it was clear she had lymphoma and was dying, I also became aware of the nature of ethical debates. Should the parents bankrupt themselves to take Mary home? Was it worth risking the flight? When should Mary's frail grandpa learn the truth? And finally, is anyone wronged if Mary's parents now hope for another child? It has been nearly three years and I still lack answers, but I now better understand the role human relations play in decision making.

My friendship with Mary continues to resurface in elements of my life and in my interactions with others. I am now more appreciative of things and try to experience enough for us both. On top of my formal course load, I now regularly audit other interesting classes on topics ranging from the U.S. Civil War to German Romanticism. While I stayed almost entirely on campus freshman year, as a sophomore I began to explore downtown Philly—and to take my shyer friends with me so they, too, would not miss out. By being attentive to details like professors' birthdays and the favorite movies of our security guard's grandchildren, and by becoming conscious of someone's state of mind by his behavior, I am able to understand and connect with others on a deeper and more rewarding level than I could have ever before. Perhaps I only knew Mary for one year, but she has given me the lessons of a lifetime. I will never forget her.

Analysis

This essay's strength lies in its revelation of the applicant's character. Jacqueline Yue, through a powerful personal anecdote, reveals her thoughtfulness, compassion, and ability to connect with others.

Woven throughout are examples of the strength of her bond with her friend Mary, as well as examples of the lessons she learned from the challenges Mary's illness posed—lessons about friendship, sacrifice, and life in general.

A personal statement like this one could be risky if not crafted carefully. After all, a friend—not the applicant—is its central focus. But the experience described was clearly formative for Yue, shaping her perspective on human relationships and making her more appreciative of what life has to offer. And Yue's approach is nuanced: She manages to convey a great deal about herself (importantly, without seeming callous or trivializing Mary's situation).

Yue points out that she wrestled with ethical dilemmas when Mary's death began to seem inevitable. And while addressing moral questions is a large part of what lawyers do, the candidate leaves it to the admissions officer to infer her reason(s) for wanting to attend law school. Yue might have improved the strength of her essay—and had room to elaborate on her legal interest, specifically—by condensing the description of her interaction with Mary. The story she's telling is poignant and compelling, but she ought to have explained how this experience inspired her interest in pursuing a legal career. Applicants should avoid making her main mistake: It's important to make the law school's admissions officers want you, but equally important to prove that you want them.

Still, Yue's essay reveals her loyalty, reliability, and mature perspective. It is clear that she would be an asset to the school's intellectual community; it also seems likely that she would put her law degree to use in the service of others.

—Lisa Mogilanski

SARAH O'LOUGHLIN

Alison Chase is an innovator in modern dance. Artistic director and choreographer of Pilobolus—a world-renowned dance company known for its intertwining of dance, acrobatics, and spectacle— Alison Chase has had a profound impact on the aesthetic development of modern dance. But Alison Chase's name will not be found in a program, on a playbill, or the company's website; her legacy has been stripped. When Chase left the company in 2005 in response to a management redirection, she simultaneously abandoned all rights and legal ownership to her own creative work. The dances belonged to the company, not to her.

After hearing Chase's story, I was outraged by her inability to hold onto something she herself had created. It's disturbing and unimaginable to me that our laws struggle to protect the abstract property that is increasingly molding and infiltrating our society. In an ever-advancing technological age more and more of ourselves, our thoughts, and our creations exist outside of us in an intangible form that requires strong legal protection. This story, and too many others like it, have cemented my passion to develop and reform the ways our laws approach and preserve the ownership of abstract intellectual property.

A dancer myself since the age of two, I have grown to hold a unique perspective toward the abstract and the creative, toward the idea of physical bounds and our abilities to harness them. Many of the hours I have spent in the dance studio have focused on taking a conceptual idea and transforming it into something the audience can feel and see—something very real and concrete. Through this constant effort to physically manifest an idea, I have developed a distinct comprehension of the intangible.

Once while playing a game in my sixth-grade English class that involved deciding whether a given object was abstract or concrete, I argued against my teacher's answer when I insisted that my object, light, should be placed within the concrete category. To this day I stand by my position. Light can be quantified. It can be measured, controlled, and changed, thereby rendering it a definitive and palpable entity. I strongly believe that this unique lens through which I approach immaterial objects and ideas will prove a valuable tool in my pursuit to develop new ways of assessing and protecting intellectual and abstract property in our legal system.

While dance has allowed me to open and expand my perspectives, it has also taught me the importance of real and concrete application. In a performance my senior year, one particular dance required pantomiming various body parts "falling off" and being reattached throughout the piece. When a preshow review described the dancers' tooth reinsertion as "putting objects into their mouths," the majority of the cast became enraged at the misrepresentation of the piece's meaning. While they spent the afternoon drafting a letter to the article's author, I returned to the dance studio to practice securing my front tooth into place. Sitting alone in front of the mirror, I remember feeling slightly ridiculous for putting so much effort and fuss into one small, quick, and seeming inconsequential move. Still, I knew it was the accuracy and exactness of this tiny gesture that would transform the piece into something the audience could grasp and understand; without this meticulous dedication to each movement and moment within the piece, the choreographer's vision and intention would be lost.

Dance has taught me the fundamental value of detail and precision. This is what allows abstract and creative ideas to translate into real time and space, thereby becoming concrete. My years spent studying and performing both the physical and intellectual components of modern dance have taught me to merge intention with creativity—to test the limits of our imagination, while striving for accuracy of execution that will make those ideas come to life. It is through this balance between idea and application that I have found success as a dancer and student, and I eagerly anticipate utilizing this perspective in my law career.

Modern dance is about boundlessness; it pushes you to explore the undiscovered possibilities of the human body in its ability to move, create, and express. For me, law is hardly different. Building from set precedents, the law is constantly changing, evolving, and becoming anew. As I look to begin my legal career, I find that my dance training has not only cultivated and enriched my views toward legal policy, but also prepared me to take on the rigor and dedication that comes with the study and practice of law.

Analysis

Sarah O'Loughlin's personal statement demonstrates her ability to connect with people through the law, and not just because of the law. Her zest for justice goes beyond the rhetoric and dives into real cases that are a consequence of our legal system. It is clear that she doesn't want to just practice law, she wants to shape it through practice. By indicating that she plans to use her skillset to advance a greater cause, she does not merely pause at the surface. She highlights the tools she has mastered in order to approach the law from a seemingly novel standpoint and thus O'Loughlin brings to the forefront the contributions she stands to make to law. It is important to demonstrate that you not only want to learn from the law but you also intend to impact it.

At times, O'Loughlin's narrative runs into trouble. For instance, her sixth-grade anecdote about classifying light is unclear and out of place. She aims to convey a capacity for understanding and making real otherwise abstract concepts. But she already makes that point with her dancing metaphor. The idea that an isolated comment from sixth grade connects with a broader orientation at life is tenuous on its face. Here, the anecdote—a shift from the broader story of dancing—feels heavy-handed, as if scripted after the fact.

Taking a wider perspective of the essay, it also makes a somewhat sudden shift from the intellectual questions of intellectual property raised in the context of dance to the extended metaphor of O'Loughlin's own dancing. O'Loughlin introduces important questions early on, hinting at a broader motivation, but she never circles back to fully explain her motivation for attending

Later in the essay, the cornerstone is O'Loughlin's ability to run the same theme and concept through various parts of her argument. Each aspect is threaded together to elucidate the different dimensions that contribute to her bid for admission. It is critical that your personal statement not only illustrates your interest in law but also tells a narrative about who you are as a whole applicant. It should not just be a composite list of accomplishments directly relevant to law school. Use your personal statement to say what the rest of your application cannot.

—Mandi Nyambi

RACHEL E. ENDICK

Ben had just turned eleven when he was found in a state park holding a bag of marijuana. It was 9:30 on a Wednesday night in May. An officer on a routine patrol of the grounds smelled the distinctive odor of the burning substance, and it led him directly to Ben, who was under a tree with the bag in one hand and a stick in the other. He was all alone.

I crossed paths with Ben during the summer that I was an intern at the OPD (Office of the Public Defender) of New Jersey. Though I spent the majority of my time working with adult criminal defendants—many of them inside the county jail—I could not resist taking on Ben's juvenile case the day he was due in court. His mother had refused repeated attempts by various OPD investigators to have Ben interviewed, leaving us with nothing but the police report. My curiosity was piqued by the odd fact pattern and his mother's refusal to cooperate, the latter of which meant that Steve, the attorney dedicated to juvenile matters, would only have time for a brief chat with Ben before presenting his case. As we drove to the courthouse, I had a clear mental image of Ben, the precocious rebel. Instead, Steve and I found a terrified child who refused to make eye contact. His mother, grandparents, and stepfather surrounded him. Every question that Steve and I asked was swiftly met with a response by Ben's stepfather, who, prior to answering, would squeeze Ben on the shoulder. Something was clearly amiss.

Steve told Ben's family that we needed a few minutes alone with Ben, and Ben's stepfather begrudgingly exited with the rest of his entourage. Ben sat with his hands in his lap and refused to speak until Steve explained the concept of attorney-client privilege in such a way that a child could grasp it. With that the floodgates opened. We learned that Ben had been given the marijuana to hold by a group of teenagers who instantly fled the park, likely because they spotted the officer. More importantly, however, we learned that Ben ran to the park that night to escape the routine abuse he suffered at the hands of his stepfather.

Steve and I flanked Ben as we walked into the courtroom. Immediately, Steve asked for a moment in chambers with the prosecutor, leaving me alone in the courtroom with Ben and his family. Ben's stepfather demanded the details of our conversation. Ben looked up at me, clearly terrified, and his expression said one thing—help me. Called upon to improvise, I began tapping my figurative heels in double-time.

I quickly explained that Ben had done a phenomenal job of relaying how he had become a scapegoat on the night in question and that Steve was seeing whether the charges could be dropped. It seemed plausible, but I could not take the chance that Ben would feel pressured to relay any other portion of our conversation. Justifying the move as procedural, I steered Ben to the defense counsel table and placed him in the chair farthest from his family. The guard sauntered over from his post at the bench to ask if there was a problem. I furtively shot my eyes toward Ben's stepfather. The guard silently nodded, left the courtroom, and soon reappeared with two other guards. One took the post by the bench, one stood in front of Ben's stepfather, and my new friend positioned himself next to my chair, providing yet another barrier between Ben and his abuser. The guards and I looked at each other in silence, and, out of the corner of my eye, I saw Ben's stepfather grow restless. I had no idea how much longer Steve would be. Finally, desperate to mask the gravity of the situation, I blurted out, "So how about those Yankees?" The guards took turns chiming in, and I, frankly with little of value to contribute, threw in generic phrases of agreement every so often. At that moment the guards and I rivaled the company of Riverdance.

After what seemed like hours Steve, the prosecutor, and the judge emerged. The charges against Ben were dropped, and the judge issued a protective order against Ben's stepfather, who was escorted out of the courthouse. Heartbreakingly, Ben's mother chose to leave with her husband, instead of remaining with her son. Nevertheless, Ben left with his grandparents who vowed to keep him out of harm's way, and Steve assured Ben that he had done well.

I left the courthouse that day with an immense feeling of gratitude that Steve and I had managed to keep Ben safe. Still, I was frustrated that the most I could do for Ben was rely on my limited knowledge of the law and my ability to think on my feet. Though my courtroom tap dance managed to be successful, I never again wanted to be in a position in which the well-being of any person relied upon an action with such little foundation in the substance of the law. The law is an inimitable tool for protecting the most vulnerable members of society, and I look forward to using it as such.

Analysis

This essay finds its strength in its counterintuitive focus on someone other than Rachel Endick. Readers become tied up in the drama and pathos of Ben's story, trusting her to guide them through the rescue of this young man. As such, she has shifted focus from their own desires and needs, and instead focused their attention on a case that illustrates Endick's prowess and ability to think on her feet. This allows her to reveal her strengths without sounding presumptuous or arrogant.

As important as what Endick says is how she says it. The essay winds through its anecdote with many of the techniques a short story or novel might employ. It has a clear, compelling plot. It is suspenseful. Most of all, it draws the readers into her mind and emotions and thought process. The personal statement isn't a hermetically sealed form of writing. It can and should employ a variety of techniques and styles. She clearly understands that.

Finally, it's important to notice that Endick doesn't mention a specific law school, or even her desire to attend law school, until the final paragraph. This is, of course, not a hard-and-fast rule to follow, but in this essay it plays well, allowing the story to speak for itself. Endick has cast herself as a character in a larger story about the justice system, and as such has made an implicit promise that law and education are central to her point, even though she doesn't explicitly mention them. Her final decision to segue into law school with the admittance of her own lack of experience is a bold one, but, again, in this particular essay it works well because she does so in the context of real life experience, thereby promising that, while she is green, she is inspired to learn.

—*Sorrel Nielsen*

JOHN

It had never occurred to me to learn to box, let alone in Cairo. But the Russian Cultural Center, a converted villa with a small boxing gym, had always been an intriguing sight on my way to Arabic class. One weeknight in winter 2009, without completely knowing where my feet were taking me, I stepped into the humid, windowless main room of the gym in search of a challenge. My eyes darted between cracked punching pads duct-taped to the walls and a gnarled pull-up bar bolted high above the hard brown floor. My heart started pumping faster than it normally did, even in the crowded streets of Cairo.

I extended a clammy hand to the gym's head coach, Sadeer, a svelte Tajik who spoke no English and little Arabic and who seemed to have a murky past. As he bounced between me and the primarily Egyptian gym clientele, jerking bodies around to correct stances while bellowing broken words of encouragement, I began to feel invigorated. Sadeer was hard to connect with, but his style also left no room for inhibition. Many of the gym's members dwarfed my 5'10", 155-pound frame, but as I pushed through that first workout I began to feel my head clearing and my endorphins flowing.

As I continued coming to the gym, I felt a momentum building. Sadeer's fitness routine emphasized what is gospel for good boxers: a strong core, quick reflexes, and endurance. Running had been my only exercise ever since high school, so a lot of this was unfamiliar and painful territory. But I found myself embracing the pain, even inviting more of it, in a way that the promise of a good mile time had never inspired me to do. As I got in better shape and learned the basic boxing moves, I started itching to spar inside the ring for the first time.

After a few weeks, Sadeer finally let me. It did not go well. Learning the basics had been hard enough, but suddenly someone else was in my face, having followed the same routine and learned the same moves as I had! Suddenly I had to think about much more than my own ability to throw punches. As we danced around each other, arms extending and retracting, feet shuffling, and bodies dripping with sweat, the confusion of it all got the better of me. I got hit.

I started reeling. The shock was more disorienting than anything, but the punch had also knocked my jaw slightly out of place. Sadeer came over to me, and with a towel wrapped around his hand, reached inside my mouth, grabbed me by the jaw, pulled, and popped it back into place. As he saw the disappointment and frustration in my eyes, he put his thumb and four fingers together in the classic Egyptian gesture that means, "slow down." "*Sabrak,*" he said in Arabic. Be patient.

I went home that day feeling defeated. But I saw the truth in Sadeer's words as the weeks went along. Jumping into the ring, I realized, was not nearly as important as taking time to build the skills I needed once inside it. As much of a rush as it was to strap on gloves and trade punches with someone else, I did my most important learning at less than half that speed, bare-handed, honing my form and footwork over and over again in front of a mirror or face-to-face with Sadeer.

Boxing in Cairo taught me a lot about the confidence, patience, and perseverance that I need in order to have the Middle East–related career I have long desired. But it has also helped me think about why I want that career to be in the law, and to start at Harvard. I think our country's engagements with the Middle East are too much about trading punches in the ring, and not enough about refining our strategies before we cross over the ropes in the first place. The law offers the richest and most nuanced set of tools for engaging the region according to our interests, but often we are too concerned with scoring political points or maintaining vague principles to focus on making those tools most helpful.

I want to help change this reality by exploring creative new legal approaches to terrorism, national security, and economic relationships amid a changing Middle East. To do so, I must take a step outside the "ring" that I now occupy and take time to build my knowledge of and skills in the law. I know that spending that time at Harvard will enable me to contribute much more to the fight than just punches the next time I strap on a pair of gloves.

Analysis

John's essay highlights the author's unique approach to legal practice and long-term ambitions for a presumptive law degree, using careful attention to detail and an elongated anecdote about boxing to highlight his pursuit for justice.

The author begins in first-person narrative, chronicling his passage in downtown Cairo to a small boxing gym that had caught his eye as he headed to his Arabic class. A lifelong runner, John keys in on the adversarial nature of boxing immediately and the aggressive loneliness of the ring. He embraces the pain and adversity and for the first time is introduced to his combative nature, a subtle undertone in the boxing anecdote that rears its head later when discussing his legal goals.

John's experience in the ring is brief; fighting for the first time, his inexperience and nervousness overwhelm his instincts and a quick punch from his opponent dislocates his jaw. The painful experience focuses the essay and brings the reader to the story's theme: The reward was in the training, not the fight.

John uses this to effectively move to discuss his future. He emphasizes how boxing taught him the need for confidence, patience, and perseverance—qualities that led him to pursue Harvard Law School. Rarely do essays draw morals as effectively from their stories and John is able to quickly turn this anecdote into a referendum on U.S. policy in the Middle East.

The pivot in the penultimate paragraph allows John to lay out a comprehensive and original plan for combating terrorism. Extending his metaphor to trading "punches" with terrorists is a tad overdone. After such a strong buildup, these lines feel uncharacteristically weak. Still, his clear language in this section enables him to make the rare move from anecdote to global policy proposal.

In short essays, it is rare for a writer to so quickly extrapolate and effectively lessons from his past. John chooses a unique experience—the combative solitude of a boxer—to epitomize the qualities he has adopted as he heads to law school. He does this with a story that is neither trite or cliché; his unique perspective and focused conclusion clearly conveys his motivation for getting into Harvard Law. The original tack he takes, culminated with a focused, unique legal mission, differentiates this essay from others of its ilk.

—David Freed

ROYALCROWN

I wake up to a call from the Student Life office at two in the morning and start my walk across campus. Fifteen minutes later and I'm ready to go, cup of coffee in hand. Most newspaper production nights end like this—we have until four in the morning to send our manuscripts to the press, and scrambling to meet deadlines is a way of life. As a senior editor, I have the luxury of taking a nap at midnight until I am needed, and I'm needed about every production night. I take my two hours gratefully.

But this night is different. Normally, I have to copyedit a last-minute draft, or approve a controversial article. Tonight, there is no draft at all. A columnist told the editor-in-chief an hour ago that he just couldn't get his article submitted in time. This meant I would be charged with filling up half a page of content in a span of two hours. I waste no time heading straight to the library, the only building still open on campus.

The article slated to run tomorrow concerns a lawsuit. A 2011 alumnus had created a Tumblr page mocking public relations photos released by Washington University. The University claimed that the student had violated copyright laws by using its name and photos. The former student argued that his blog fell under Fair Use and thus was protected. Both sides claim that they have the right of the issue, so I need to find out more. The article's topic strikes me as particularly interesting, since I have never covered a story concerning a legal topic in the past. Ideally, I would like to know if either side's claims have any merit. Thankfully for me, Washington University students don't sleep, and I have my pick of late-night crammers to interview. By the end of the interviews, it was clear that no consensus emerged from polling the students. Nearly everyone had an opinion, and each one was different. The responses were varied:

"The whole point of a parody is to copy the original as much as possible in order to make fun of the original expression," said one. "The University is simply protecting against unauthorized use of their images, and are not trying to 'bully the little guy,'" said another. Then a simple solution, "Why doesn't Wash. U. just get rid of those dumb pictures that appear on the website anyway?"

Though I failed at getting any concrete answers from the student body, their comments leave an impact on me. While some students made a moral claim, justifying the actions of one side, others advanced concrete solutions to the problem at hand, without making an evaluative claim. But as a journalist, I need something decisive. I try in vain to contact a University representative, but nobody is up at this hour. I return to the library with forty-five minutes to spare and nothing to show for my efforts.

As I walk back in, I notice a man several years older than any undergraduate, wearing a suit at three in the morning, with what appear to be legal briefs on the table in front of him. He turns out to be an Adjunct Professor of Law at the University, and a prime candidate for some answers. He speculates that the University is likely to make a Digital Millennium Copyright Act claim. Instead of pursuing the student directly, the University would instead target Tumblr, who could be held liable under the law if they are found to be hosting a web page that illegally makes use of copyrighted materials. "I'm personally just disappointed that it's going to be taken down," he tells me. "I think it's actually useful to have a website that openly mocks the student experience at Wash. U. That's something that people can really be open about and reflect on. This is a place where we share ideas, and the University has presumably come in and tried to shut that off."

I make it back to the office at 3:30 A.M. and pound out a draft, which the editor-in-chief gratefully accepts and begins editing. The article will be published in her name, but I don't mind—I'm just thankful to go back to bed and catch another couple of hours of sleep before class. Besides, I have something else on my mind. As I walk back to campus, dawn just starting to break, I can't help but think about how the professor I'd met had been so convinced that the website would be taken down, and yet personally advocated its existence anyway.

As a philosophy major, I often find myself contemplating the right solution to an ethical dilemma. I just as often speculate on what might actually happen given an ethical dilemma, most often in the form of thought experiments involving trolleys. Rarely do I get the opportunity to think about where those two paths intersect. I notice myself becoming intrigued by this overlap between the reasons for and against a given issue, on the one hand, and the various ways in which a winner and a loser are ultimately decided. As I get under the covers and close my eyes, I find myself unable to sleep. I'm still thinking about the article. It wouldn't be my first all-nighter, so I get back up, brew another cup of coffee, and head to my computer. I fire up Google and start to look into law schools. I'm already fascinated.

Analysis

Anecdotes can be an effective way to communicate positive qualities about oneself in an essay without making it sound like a résumé. Instead of saying "I am passionate about the law" or "I am a hardworking person," the author uses a central anecdote to communicate all of this and more. When Harvard Law School admissions officers read this essay, they immediately know that the author is willing to lose sleep in order to meet his commitments. They know that he is not afraid to seek out strangers and do the type of research and investigating that is crucial to the law practice. They also know exactly how the law fascinated him and why he decided to apply to HLS.

These are all qualities that are not always easy to communicate, but through this anecdote, the author does so effectively. By using short, concrete sentences and quotes from colleagues to advance the narrative, the essay never feels dry. Instead, every sentence plays an important role in painting an image for the admissions officer. The story essentially tells itself. The author does not explicitly refer to himself outside the context of this one, early morning, but that is also reason why his essay works so well. By not having to step out of character, he maximizes the one-thousand-word limit and allows the narrative to make the argument.

The essay is an applicant's best opportunity to stand out as more than a number on a page. For applicants struggling to communicate their reasons for applying to HLS, an anecdote may be the answer. Instead of talking about yourself, let the story speak for you. Perhaps there was a court case or a conversation with a professor that sparked your interest in law, just as it did for the author. In that case, an anecdote may be the key to your successful HLS application.

—Dennis Ojogho

JOHN WHEELER

It's 6:53 on a Monday evening. My three-hour shift at Vanderbilt's Writing Studio starts in seven minutes. As I set my backpack down at my favorite table, I hope for a few minutes to sit, to check my e-mail, to relax. No luck. The client walks through the door right after me: a short, dark-haired girl, impossibly cheerful considering it's getting close to finals week. I smile, introduce myself, and ask her about her paper. She tells me the basics: when it's due, how long it is, how long it's supposed to be, what she wants to work on. *Flow*, she says, which is a shorter word for *everything*.

The paper, I quickly realize, is good. Too good, it seems at first. How am I supposed to know what *deracination* means this late in the evening? The real problem isn't the vocabulary, though; it's the complexity. She's got enough insightful ideas in her intro to fuel ten thesis statements. Naturally, she's interested in all of them. For the next fifty minutes, it's my job to help her pare them down to what's both necessary and sufficient for this paper. In other words, I need to help her make the paper flow.

I start off, as I often do, with a Moment of Panic. It consists of the standard question—*How am I going to do this?!*—plus a couple of existential quandaries (*Why am I here? Who in their right mind thought I belonged here?*). Fortunately, the moment never lasts long, and it takes place in the back of my mind, leaving me free to keep the session going. The answer to the standard question is the same every time: Break it down. Break down the ideas, break down the sentences, break down the arguments into basic logical progressions. Whenever something seems problematic or confusing, break it down.

We fuse her ideas into what she considers the core of her argument—a working thesis, I like to call it. She writes it down: a single sentence, long but clear. She'll probably change it as we get through more of the paper, but for now, we have a direction. We move to the body paragraphs and evaluate the strength of the topic sentences, analyze the relationship of evidence to analysis, follow the reasoning from one sentence to the next. At some point, I become absorbed. Eventually, my brain snaps me out of it enough for me to glance at the clock. "Crap!" I think. "We're almost out of time." I say it out loud, except for the *crap* part, and inwardly I cringe: We've covered exactly half of her six-page paper. That's all.

She doesn't mind. She thanks me and says it's been helpful. I smile. We go over the biggest takeaways: Make sure those topic sentences really encompass the argument. Break down those logical chains as much as you need to. Bullet points, even. Just make sure you're not skipping steps.

And I'm happy. We didn't talk about the whole paper, but she's left with something new, a handful of ideas on how to make the paper into what she wants it to be. And that's enough. That's what I'm here for. Now I remember, as I do at the end of almost every session, why I love this job. At the Writing Studio, I can help people, truly and immediately. I can spend fifty minutes with them, and even if we don't get through the whole paper, even if we don't work through everything they're concerned about, I know that they leave happier than they came in.

This is what appeals to me about law school: the idea of using what I know, what I'm good at, to help people. Writing. Argumentation. Logic. Analysis. My grade school and college careers have taught me these skills, and I want to make sure that I put them to the best use possible. I'm not sure yet what type of law I want to practice, or what legal area interests me the most, but I'm confident that all of them will offer me the opportunity to build on my skills and to use them for the good of other people. And *that*, I believe, is what I'm here for.

Analysis

Notice how far along John Wheeler gets in this essay before even mentioning the words "law school." Admissions officers know why you are writing, so don't worry about your framing your essay at the beginning—jump right into your story.

And when you tell whichever story you choose, tell it, as Wheeler does. His essay evokes confidence because he clearly is not worried about spending every word promoting himself. He sets a scene, and in fact ends up talking almost as much about somebody else as he does himself. That's fine. There are several other places to list your accomplishments and abilities; you don't need to do it again in the essay. Instead, use the essay to build an implicit argument that amplifies your list of accomplishments. Certainly, Wheeler has plenty of extracurricular activities that display his proclivity for helping others, but this essay will make those stand out when the admissions officer goes back over Wheeler's résumé. It also shows that he truly enjoys helping others rather than just doing those things to pad his résumé or make an extra dollar.

Wheeler displays his confidence again in the final paragraph, admitting that he isn't sure what type of law he wants to practice. He is willing to show his true self and does not attempt to hide uncertainty and doubt. Yet, he shows no doubt about his desire to practice law or his motivations for that desire. He is also very clear and up-front in the final paragraph. While much of the rest of the essay is focused on details, he closes with broad statements about his past experience and future ambitions, conveying his belief that he belongs in law school. These kinds of broad strokes wouldn't be effective if they were deployed throughout an essay, but they work quite well as an explanation of the story Wheeler opened with.

It can be difficult to portray confidence without coming off as fake, but it's a place worth pursuing. Wheeler finds that spot by using a story to make an implicit argument before digressing into a broader discussion of his past, all the while not getting caught up in his accomplishments or hiding instances of uncertainty.

—*Jacob Feldman*

JOEL KNOPF

Last November, I taught my friend Madeleine how to tone. We entered the cavernous stone interior of Dwight Chapel. No choir stood poised to sing its first note; no audience murmured in the wooden pews. There was only the echo of footsteps as Madeleine and I passed between tall granite pillars to the far end of the hall. We were standing a pace from each other by the altar when I began to sing. My improvised jig reverberated through the space. Catching Madeleine's eye, I invited her to make up a melody to match mine. We were trying to create a coherent harmony from two independently improvised lines, but our harmonies sounded jangly and disconnected. We were not toning; we were just two people singing to ourselves.

We began again by soaking in the silence. Very quietly, we practiced singing the same pitch until the chapel replied with one voice. We tuned two pitches until their overtones rang from wall to wall. Once, when we were tuning two notes a fourth apart, I caught Madeleine's eye and inclined my head. She moved her note down a step, gingerly resolving the fourth to a sweet major third. It was our first harmony.

Improvising extended harmonies was harder because we didn't know which notes the other person would sing next. Madeleine looked to me when she was lost. My furrowed brow signaled an upcoming dissonance; a tilted chin said to change notes now. Gradually, we learned to fashion our lines into a conversation: I held a note, and she filled in my line with ornamentation; Madeleine's scurrying eighth notes called forth a quick burst of melody from me. On our best days, harmonies flowed from one to the next as if we were reading from a score. Eyes twinkling, Madeleine and I would smile even when our voices clashed, because we knew we could resolve our dissonances together.

We became musical mind readers. The intentions and desires of another person can seem as opaque as a musical score is to a novice musician. Yet Madeleine and I had a richer experience because we strove to understand each other's intentions and harmonize with them.

As a student of cognitive science, I know that music is not the only means for minds to meet. I can bridge minds with my stories, and reduce cognitive dissonance with my words. Nor are singers the only ones who resolve clashes by listening to others' perspectives, responding to their interests, and adapting when expectations are upended.

Madeleine once surprised me by singing some of the lush French harmonies she had been exploring on her harp. She watched for my signal to end the sudden dissonance, but I stood still. Our notes kept clashing. Finally, when she understood that I was waiting for her to lead, she relaxed, and gave a confident nod. Our lines unrolled into a cadence. The chapel kept ringing even after our voices had fallen silent.

Analysis

In this essay the candidate explores the ways in which two individuals can negotiate and reconcile their differences through music. The extended metaphor used in this essay works well; the candidate successfully relates his enthusiasm for music, cognitive science, and writing to a common desire to bridge dissimilarities and overcome conflict.

Joel Knopf opens the essay with a detailed description of the chapel and the singing instruction he gives Madeleine. Through this anecdote we learn that Knopf is a skilled singer, an enthusiastic teacher, a patient friend, and a reflective writer. He conveys both his interests and his personality, painting a picture of himself in a moment in time.

Though Knopf's flowery literary style is impressive, it distracts a bit from the central message of the essay, which is not revealed until the very end. The essay may have been stronger with a more thorough exploration of the relationship between cognitive science, music, and words—the moment when Knopf gestures at the similarities between singing in a chapel and practicing law. Though Knopf plays on the parallelisms of cognitive and musical dissonance, the subject could be discussed in more depth. By tightening the lengthy descriptions of improvisational harmonizing, Knopf may have been able to better connect the dots between his musical passion and his desire to communicate across difference and empower others to lead.

The moment Knopf describes is perhaps not one of his biggest achievements, yet he examines the deeper meaning in the activities of his daily life, giving the reader the sense that he is thoughtful and purposeful in all that he does. The essay's case could be more explicit, but its point carries through: Knopf's ability to respond quickly to changing circumstances and his eagerness to make room for diverse perspectives are as relevant to legal work as they are to musical improvisation

—*Zoe A. Y. Weinberg*

NIMRA AZMI

The sky was still dark—but it was almost dawn. I tightened my sweat-sticky headscarf. Watching the men circumambulating the sacred black stone of the Kaaba in Mecca, Saudi Arabia, I could not help but envy their *ehrams*, white towels that draped around their waists like airy togas.

I had come to Saudi Arabia with my family to perform the Umrah, an Islamic pilgrimage that can be best described as an abbreviated version of the obligatory Hajj. Pilgrimage, whether it be Hajj or Umrah, is meant to be a great equalizer. Men dress in identical *ehrams* and women garb themselves plainly. Race or class do not matter. Men and women are not supposed to be segregated. We are all equal in our worship of Allah.

Men and women sat in patches, hugging the black and gilded Kaaba, waiting for the call to the Fajr prayer on my final day in Mecca. Legs folded beneath me, I watched the Saudi *shurta*—civil police officers—divide the women and the men. "Very well then," I thought equably. "Separate but equal." As I looked on, groups of women worshippers were being pushed back from the Kaaba by the *shurta*. Initially, I assumed the officers were creating space for more worshippers, men and women alike. I quickly realized that women were being forced back to make room for more men, as if the prayer of men took precedence over the prayer of women, as if they deserved to pray closer to the Kaaba by virtue of their gender. There is no Islamic injunction, legal or otherwise, that states women must yield their places before the Kaaba to men. No, it was merely man-made tradition that perpetuated this prejudice. I was incensed. All semblance of spiritual calm evaporated.

A *shurta* approached where I sat with my mother and a dozen other unknown women. "Move," he said in Arabic. I pretended not to understand. "Move," he tried again in English. "*Je ne comprends pas*," I answered. Turning away, he tried to bully the other women into leaving. A few departed. More stayed. He returned, but I ignored him, staring blandly at the soaring marble minarets above. Angrily, the *shurta* shoved me.

In worried Urdu, my mother said, "We should leave. They could put you in jail."

I looked at the surrounding space, once almost evenly distributed between men and women, but now overtaken by men at the behest of the Saudi officers. I would not be bullied into surrendering my religious rights, I decided—especially not when my intention was shared by the ten or so women around me. I shook my head. "You can go, but I'm going to pray here."

An old woman, her brown face lined by the sun, turned to me. "It is almost Fajr; they cannot make you move once the *imam* calls for prayer. Sit and wait." She gripped my hand, the papery-soft pads of her fingers digging into my palm. I cannot remember how we communicated. She did not speak English and I only knew the most rudimentary classical Arabic. But her meaning was clear: Resist patiently. Dawn will come and they cannot stop us then.

She was right. Despite the attempts of the *shurta*, as the sun rose and the call to prayer wove through the air, we prayed side by side, two women disparate in age, language, and nationality, but who had prevailed over one small injustice together.

This happened six months before the Arab Spring burst forth in Tunisia. In Saudi Arabia, at the holiest place in Islam, through that woman, I saw a kernel of that spirit and took heart from it. That same spirit drives me to pursue a legal education to advocate for a feminist reinterpretation of Islamic law. Women around the world may have had their rights usurped by men operating under the veil of religion, but many of these women are neither unaware nor nonresistant. It is the kind of quiet strength displayed by that woman in Saudi Arabia that I wish to work with following law school as a proponent for women's rights in the Muslim world.

Analysis

A good story makes can make for a great personal statement, and Nimra Azmi's essay hits the mark. Narrative structure keeps the pages turning and can effectively convey personal strengths. Writing your own essay, it's important to think hard about the story you want to tell. What does it show about you as a law school candidate? Azmi's essay not only demonstrates her superb writing skills, it also illustrates her dedication, values, and passion for a specific branch of law—women's rights in the Muslim world.

Azmi uses sensory description and action verbs to immediately immerse readers in the world of her essay. She makes sure to define words and concepts that may be unfamiliar to an admissions officer. Writing about religion can sometimes be tricky, but Azmi sidesteps any potential offense by straightforwardly describing the pilgrimage and Muslim beliefs.

Suspense builds as Azmi describes how the police officer hassled her—an anecdote that maintains reader interest and shows Azmi's commitment to her goals. The moment when the old woman takes Azmi's hand is a nice touch, beautifully written and shows that Azmi understands the values of patience and silence. Again, detailed and clear writing help Azmi take a single, foundational incident from her life and extrapolate its relevance to her future law career.

Throughout her essay, Azmi draws the reader in with her well-flowing account. But it isn't just a well-flowing account. It isn't just a good story. More than that, it shows what kind of person Azmi is—a person who is resilient, brave, and intelligent. And it shows them without bragging. Instead, the reader finds oneself rooting for Azmi. And by taking time to reflect on the anecdote at the essay's close, Azmi adds a layer of thoughtfulness onto the qualities already displayed. Put all of that together, and you have a strong law school candidate, and one with a clear, forward-looking focus. Her compelling story illustrates strong motivations and impressive passion for a law career in global women's rights.

—*Julia F. P. Ostmann*

IDENTITY

Who are you? Any good personal statement should answer that question, but identity can be approached in a variety of ways, as these essays show. Some writers draw from their identities, others seek to grow beyond them, and still others search for identity in the first place. All tell admissions officers something important about the applicant.

The concept of your identity encompasses a lot—from your heritage to your upbringing to your own ideas and actions. But don't let your essay sprawl by trying to answer everything in a few hundred words. In general, the essays in this section don't merely itemize authors' identities; instead, they follow the theme of identity in unique directions. One uses a multicultural background to inform views on global social issues. One describes the examination of identity in the midst of coming out as gay. One surveys socioeconomic challenges through the lens of a small-town emigrant.

None of the essays attempts to lay out a complete blueprint of who the author is, and a strong identity-based essay shouldn't make its analysis explicit. Instead, keep your writing closely tied to your experiences, and let those experiences tell an admissions officer who you really are.

AMANDA MOREJON

One night seven years ago, my mother and I sat in the car waiting for the light to change when a homeless man knocked on our window. This was not the first time such an event had occurred and yet I became especially saddened by his presence. It was not just this man's predicament that upset me, but rather the combination of events that transpired that day. In my high school history class, we had discussed slavery in America and the atrocities of the Holocaust. That evening I had attended the Hudson County Child Abuse Prevention Center meeting, which highlighted an increase in child abuse in the area. And now a homeless person was begging for money. My sadness as a naïve fifteen-year-old Afro-Cuban teenager came to inform my proactive stance and future view of the world as a place that needed to change.

Now, seven years later sitting in my sociology class at Harvard, I listen to my classmates discuss the relative merits of assigning blame to structural factors as opposed to cultural values for the inequities in America. The consensus in my class is clear: Structural inequalities result in negative consequences for many people and so ascribing societal wrongs to cultural values is misguided. These types of conversations are particularly salient for me, as structural inequalities have had significant meaning in my own life as an Afro-Cuban woman.

For me, structural inequalities meant that I had to travel eighteen miles to attend a private high school because the public school system in my hometown of Union City, New Jersey, was deficient. While I was fortunate to attend this high school, the friends I left behind were not as lucky. Some of my former eighth-grade classmates were either pregnant within their freshmen year of high school or arrested for selling drugs. Structural inequalities meant that my best friend's father, the only Hispanic worker at his office, was fired because he was "too lazy." The manager did not realize that my friend's father had bipolar disorder and two days after being fired, he committed suicide in his family's basement. Structural inequalities meant that my parents, who both immigrated from Cuba, had to adapt quickly to their schools with different access to resources. My grandparents managed to put my mother in a Head Start program, which gave my mother opportunities that my father never received. As a result, my father was forced to repeat second grade due to his English-language deficiency. Structural inequalities meant that many of my Hispanic female friends in middle school were sexually molested by an older white male student in the after-school program. The male student, a teacher's son, suffered no consequences.

As I reflect on these situations, it becomes difficult for me, as an Afro-Cuban woman, to separate race and gender inequalities from the insidiousness of structural disparities. When we discuss structural inequalities in my sociology classes, I agree with my classmates that the "victim" is never to blame. However, discussion alone is never satisfying and I find myself spurred to action. During these past four years, I have elected to work with programs and groups that specifically focus on the empowerment of women and communities of color. This work has led me to realize that by attending law school and entering the legal profession, I will be able to have a greater impact in assisting these historically vulnerable populations. Women and people of color inordinately suffer the consequences of structural inequalities, specifically with respect to discrimination, domestic violence, harassment, sexual assault, and voter disenfranchisement.

I believe that the greatest changes in our society can occur as a result of legal and political empowerment and the passage of laws. Therefore, it is my goal to one day become an elected official and work to ensure that the rights of such vulnerable populations are protected. It is an aspiration that has been personally informed by my life's experience as an Afro-Cuban woman and person of color, and that I have cultivated in college through my intellectual pursuits and work experiences. I believe that attending law school is the first step toward combating the structural inequalities that left me hopeless just seven years ago.

Analysis

Although this essay does not start off on the strongest foot, it quickly gains in strength. Amanda Morejon begins the piece by recalling a homeless man begging on her window during her high school years. While this could potentially be a touching personal story, there is something off about it. Whereas Morejon does a good job tying other examples into her ideas of structural inequality, she leaves that example standing without relating it to her broader theme. Moving, compelling stories only help an essay if they show something important about the author and the author's message.

The opening story lacks specificity and as a result has an artificial tone. For example, Morejon simply states that she was "saddened" by the "combination of events that transpired that day"—a little more description would have gone a long way in helping the reader learn more about the person behind this personal statement. In addition, Morejon attempts to draw attention to her Afro-Cuban background and her sociology studies seem a little forced. In two occasions, she prefaces her statements with "as an Afro-Cuban woman," which is unusually jarring. The essay entirely loses this artificial touch, however, in the third paragraph. As Morejon recalls several vivid examples of structural inequality from her own life, she very effectively contrasts two sides of structural and racial inequality: that which is tackled in the classroom, and that which is encountered in everyday life. In doing so, she manages not only to stand out as an individual, but also to demonstrate a high level of maturity and of commitment to an issue that she holds very close at heart. The transition to a discussion of why she wants to be a lawyer seems very natural from there on. The essay comes full circle in the last paragraph, with a reference to the introductory story that "left [Morejon] hopeless just seven years ago."

Overall, this essay illustrates the importance of good storytelling: If you choose to recall a personal memory, make sure you fully commit yourself. Details and imagery can make all the difference between a contrived essay and a gripping narrative.

—*Sarah Fellay*

JOSH

The night everything changed is permanently stitched into the fabric of my memory. I was sitting with her at the Lincoln Memorial, gazing into her beautiful brown eyes, while the shadow of the Washington Monument bounced off the Reflecting Pool in my periphery. Her soft, almost angelic skin grazed my hand as she leaned in to whisper how she felt for me. My heart skipped a beat; my stomach sank. I stared back at her and uttered the only words that I could muster, "I have to go." As I walked away, my pace quickening with every step, I looked back only once to see her sitting there, her face drained of color, her eyes filled with tears. I felt no empathy—only relief. No despair; only pride. No confusion; only clarity. Overwhelmed, I returned to my dorm room, sat on my bed, and cried.

Two years earlier, as my junior year of high school was drawing to a close, I was preparing for the best summer of my life. After all, between the annual senior cruise, nightly parties, and countless trips around Florida, the opportunities for debauchery were endless. Yet, a constant feeling of hopelessness permeated my existence, making it the summer of my discontent. On some level I always knew I was gay, but it was at that point when the nagging feeling inside me came to a boil. I had no choice but to end the relationship with my girlfriend, my closest companion, causing a schism between us that never recovered. I withdrew from my friends and spent most nights by myself. My days were spent going through the motions, while my mind dwelled elsewhere. By the end of the summer, I was tired of feeling so dreadful. I realized that denying and camouflaging who and what I was would simply no longer suffice. After days of agonizing over the best course of action, I told my closest friends. They were more supportive than I could have imagined and helped me through one of the most difficult times of my life.

After all the progress I had made though, one choice whisked me backward. When I went to college I was given the opportunity to define myself as I wanted to be defined. Perhaps out of fear and cowardice, or perhaps because I thought I could suppress it, I went back into hiding, retreating to what seemed socially easier. On some level, I figured, who would want to be gay in a society dominated by heterosexuals? Naturally, this easy way out was far from it. Rather than allowing myself to enjoy this new and exciting experience, I fought off every impulse I had. It was as if I channeled George Costanza from that *Seinfeld* episode, where he did the exact opposite of what his instincts told him to do, only without the same hilarious results. And thus, my entire freshman year, a year that had made that earlier summer seem simple, was lost.

As the summer heat rolled in, I started to feel like I had two years prior. I was sick of the lying and of the hiding. Nevertheless, there still existed a contradiction within me that masked my real self to the outside world. In one last epic battle against myself, I called up the girl I was dating and asked if she wanted to walk with me to the Lincoln Memorial. Although I would later apologize and explain my actions to her, when she told me how she felt that night, it was as if my former self escaped my body, and I was reborn. There was not one clear reason as to why I had to leave, staying just was not an option. When I cried that night, I was not crying because I was gay. I cried because I realized just how much precious time I had wasted.

As difficult as coming out was, it paled in comparison to facing the fact that I had blown a year of college, and my life, away. In doing so, I felt as though I had lost a piece of myself. When I decided to live a facade freshman year, I failed myself in a way that I never had before. For as much as I value openness and honesty, I had lied not just to everyone else, but to myself. I consider the past two years and my ability to learn from that mistake as my greatest personal success. While my life goals and career plans have not been altered, this journey has fundamentally shifted the way that I view the world. I not only find new appreciation in the differences between myself and others, but in how each person must develop in his own time and in his own way. I realize that I will fail again in my life, but through that failure I will grow and become a better person.

Personal statements are an interesting beast; they force you to reflect upon yourself when you know there is so much left for you to achieve. They ask you to comment on who you are, while so much of you has yet to be defined. They force you to relive certain experiences, and thus in the process, reinforce and reflect upon the changes you have made in your life. It was only a few months back when I was sitting with my boyfriend on the National Mall, Abraham Lincoln gazing at me in the distance, and the Capitol Dome up ahead. His rugged hand reached to grab mine, our fingers slowly intertwining. My heart skipped a beat; my stomach sank. I leaned in and told him how I felt. He looked into my eyes and told me he felt the same way. That afternoon did not alter my life in any meaningful way. There was no sudden shift in my worldview or a new path of self-discovery to walk on. And yet, it is a memory, perhaps more than any other, which echoes the changes I have made in my life, and illustrates who I am today.

Analysis

This striking and powerful essay derives its strength from its intensely personal nature. Josh's honesty and frankness in discussing his personal failings and darkest moments is deeply moving and inspiring. He shows how, after a long process of struggle and reflection, he managed to triumph and be truthful with himself and with those around him in embracing his sexual orientation. Josh also shows how a personal experience altered his worldview and the way that he approaches life. He comes across as a thoughtful and compassionate individual who would enrich any community.

Josh opens with a semi-mysterious hook without making the mistake of keeping the reader in the dark for too long. He then quickly transitions into an explanation of his actions and the subject of his essay. He tells a story of stumbles, transformation, and resilience, without allowing the tone to become melodramatic or self-pitying. Josh takes us back to his high school days, allowing the reader to see the full arc of his journey. In returning to his moment of clarity at the Lincoln Memorial later in the essay, he achieves coherence, bringing the story full circle before discussing the most important lessons he took away from the experience.

The essay could have done without the explicit reference to the challenges of writing a personal statement. Josh has already shown himself to be reflective and self-aware, so the discussion of the act of writing a personal statement feels unnecessary. Instead, he could have transitioned immediately into the final scene at the National Mall without losing any important details. Focusing on that final scene reemphasizes one of the essay's best qualities, its compelling story and realism.

Even with that missed opportunity, the essay gives a comprehensive look at its author and his mind-set. It accomplishes that by relating a personal, seemingly myopic story and relating to show who Josh is, as well as—implicitly—casting him as a worthy applicant. This essay shows Josh's humility, introspectiveness, and how he deals with overwhelming challenges—qualities that are relevant to all aspects of life.

—*Zoe A. Y. Weinberg*

ALICIA ROBINSON

I belong to both the richest and the poorest nations of the Western Hemisphere, the United States, my mother's country of origin, and Haiti, my father's homeland. I spent ten years of my childhood and adolescence in rural Guatemala, which at the time had just emerged from a thirty-six-year civil war that resulted in the genocide of two hundred thousand Mayan indigenous people and is today rampant with drug-related violence. Together these nations represent the extremes of peace and violence, wealth and poverty, impunity and democracy. As such, the basis for my keen interest in the rule of law in different societies across the globe is precisely the fact that I know how it feels to live in a context of uncertainty and insecurity. My life experiences and the exposure to the aforementioned contrasts have proven to me that the absence of the rule of law destroys a society and propels it into a treacherous cycle of violence and poverty that affects family, neighbors, and friends.

In stark contrast to my short visits to the United States prior to attending college, the rest of my year was characterized by exposure to issues regarding forced disappearances, lynchings in the name of popular justice, human trafficking, and everyday forms of violence. My nascent interest in post-conflict societies led me to conduct a number of projects on historical memory in Spain and Guatemala during my high school and college years. My mother's work with the UN peacekeeping missions in Guatemala and Haiti had a strong impact on me and I have since pursued a number of UN internships in Geneva, Egypt, and Guatemala to broaden my understanding of the international legal and humanitarian system. It has been my ability, a true privilege in my opinion, to alternate between the realities of North and South that has granted me with a unique insight into the inherent differences between the two types of societies. My undergraduate studies at Stanford University focused on international law as a means of contextualizing my earlier life and of broadening my understanding of international and national legal frameworks as an absolutely essential character for facing these challenges.

A growing concern in the international community is the broadening gap between man and nature. The spring of my freshman year at Stanford, I sought to address the environmental and economic problems affecting the Lake Atitlán region where I grew up. I proceeded to raise $20,000 for the fuel-efficient stove initiative that I created and organized for Stanford Rotaract Club's annual project. The objective was to reduce the use of timber for fuel in order to curb the preposterous levels of deforestation, and to reduce the danger posed to women and children when exposed to open-fire cooking. The project had quantifiable results for many indigenous households and provided me with practical insight into how larger-scale environmental projects could be carried out. I also became privy to the legal aspects of such environmental issues, such as the role of government regulations and the communal rights of indigenous peoples to their cultural and historical heritage.

For the past few years, I have been unable to swim in Lake Atitlán or come into contact with the Lake's water, which provides most of the public water supply in this indigenous area. Those who do may contract various sicknesses, rashes, and parasites related to the emergence of cyanobacteria, an algae that appeared as an offset of the Lake's rising temperature and pollution. The destruction of an ecosystem, of a population's main water source, of a culturally symbolic region for the Mayan population of Guatemala has been occurring right before my eyes and efforts to curtail this phenomenon have been "too little too late." What used to be a striving tourist destination is today an economically distraught community wondering how to survive another week. It is a place that sadly reminds me of "Macondo" in One Hundred Years of Solitude by Gabriel García Márquez: a forgotten place tucked away in the mountains of Latin America, where time does not provoke fruitful change or bring about justice, and where there is no tangible future for my generation of friends.

I am someone who once attended high school in the back of an old, run-down hotel whose rooms were used as makeshift classrooms in a small indigenous town located in the highlands of Guatemala. Today, I am an individual who speaks four languages, who has traveled extensively, and who was admitted into the Phi Beta Kappa honors society as one of the Commencement speakers. My practical understanding of two major world trends leads me to approach the legal discipline with a desire to delve deeper into these issues, through studies of international and environmental law. However, I also seek to diversify my own knowledge and capabilities: I have previously been involved in different capacities with human rights, regulatory law, refugee law, and public international law, and I know that there are many more areas to explore. I have clear aspirations for my future and I envision a career that allows for mobility between both the United States and Europe. After extensive inquiry, I am committed to pursuing Harvard Law's joint JD/LLM degree with Cambridge University, for it is a great means by which to purse my objectives. It is my utmost desire to be admitted into Harvard Law School and I do hope that you will grant me the opportunity to pursue a career, which, I believe, was ultimately made for me.

Analysis

Alicia Robinson packs an impressive range of ideas into the relatively short personal statement. By integrating both interesting, dramatic anecdotes and personal insights, she is able to convey a remarkable depth of character and awareness. The essay rarely loses its focus, and every sentence serves either to deepen the reader's understanding of Robinson's past or her vision for the future.

If the structure and execution of this essay are laudable, its message is even more so. Robinson relays powerful examples of adversity she observed and faced growing up "in a context of uncertainty and insecurity," and shows deftly how her experiences have inspired and solidified her interest in the rule of law. Robinson writes: "I am someone who once attended high school in the back of an old, run-down hotel whose rooms were used as makeshift classrooms in a small indigenous town located in the highlands of Guatemala." Her childhood circumstances no doubt made her path to Stanford University, Phi Beta Kappa honors, and, ultimately, Harvard Law School more difficult than it is for most. Yet the violence and poverty she encountered did not leave her disillusioned; Robinson views these, in addition to environmental issues, as problems that can be addressed through legal frameworks.

Robinson's essay takes on a sweeping set of experiences, from her family background to her studies and internships to her travel and Lake Atitlán. As a general rule, a focused approach usually creates the best essay. Lacking that, the transitions from one idea and story to the next become all the more important. Robinson often jumps from one topic to the next without an eye for how they connect. On a related note, she closes the essay with a mechanical list of accomplishments, lacking almost any connection whatsoever. Those various points should appear in the rest of the application. Here, they come across as forced and out of place. And in an essay that already risks becoming overly broad, this listing only serves to make matters worse.

On the whole, though, Robinson shows drive, empathy, and a keen, global perspective. The essay does not feel contrived: Robinson's background and demonstrated interest in the law make the "thesis" of her personal statement highly believable. Indeed, the admissions officer gets the impression that she's the perfect fit for a career in international law (even before the candidate says so herself).

—*Lisa Mogilanski*

JORDAN KLIMEK

Having restlessly toiled behind the counter of my dad's dusty auto parts store for many years, I should have foreseen a day that I would look on my home with an outsider's eyes. That day came in April of my first year of college after I had spent four months away. I intentionally got a late start on Friday, so it was nearly ten o'clock and very cold by the time I rolled into town. The few occupied buildings on the town square were left alone for the night. My mind seized upon the image of the night wind blowing right by our little house on the north edge of town, down Grand Avenue, and past my grandpa's house on the south side of town, all without touching a piece of human civilization. With the sparkling universe looking down on that treeless, foreign town, I felt exposed, like I was on the surface of the moon.

For most of my life, my shy personality mirrored the remote nature of Burwell, Nebraska, a tiny village of 1,200 on the edge of the desolate Sandhills. I loved where I grew up, but I had a peculiar fascination from a young age with maps. Those large orange clots, big cities, were where the people were, and I always believed that I was missing out by being so far away from so many people. I just assumed that some of the quietly positive aspects of my little hometown, especially the lack of social boundaries between people of differing class or profession, were universal.

Like many of small-town America's most determined young people, I joined the premed army right away and ground my way through late nights of calculus and organic chemistry. Although my scientific education made me a more analytical thinker, I never stayed up 'til 3 A.M. reading about science (as opposed to Caro's biographies of LBJ). I puzzled my science classmates at Nebraska Wesleyan with my constant talk of tax policy or Supreme Court cases, and my outside involvement has increasingly highlighted this discrepancy. I avoided hospitals and clinics and instead chose to tutor at newly reopened Dawes Middle School. The students were very mistrustful of me at first, but we share more in common than what meets the eye. Northeast Lincoln shares one striking characteristic with Burwell. It also was left behind decades ago by a changing society. I quickly noticed the damaging effect of the spatial separation of Lincoln's children. Driving south in Lincoln is like seeing the history of the American upper middle class unfold before your eyes, street by street. South Lincoln's posh schools, one derisively termed "Von Maur High," are filled with the white children of the white-collar. By contrast, the students at Dawes are ethnically diverse, and many of them are children of immigrants, but they are deceptively homogenous as well. They are the children of convenience store clerks and forklift operators, the blue-collar. How can I convince them that they need higher education if they don't know anyone who obtained it?

Their teachers are both patient and capable, and the simple truth is that an infusion of Hollywood-style super-teachers won't solve an education crisis bred from an inequality crisis. Proactive housing and districting policies constitute the only viable path out of socioeconomic segregation for America as a whole. While I enjoy the personal interaction of teaching, I more often find myself wondering why my students don't have English textbooks, or why they are required to join a private club to play sports. The basic issue of social equity led me to pursue my policy interests through an internship at AARP last summer. My most satisfying project was a comparative state taxation study that will be used by a lobbying coalition to argue for Social Security tax relief in Nebraska. This experience confirmed my belief in the power of public policy to help vulnerable people, young and old.

I doubt I will spend the rest of my life in a courtroom, or even in a law firm. I want to attend law school because knowledge of the rules that bind society is the surest path to having the ability to shape it, and I want to meet people who have the same desire. Most of my young life has already been consumed by passion for and curiosity about the institutions like families, businesses, and schools that are bound together into a cohesive society, and I want to dedicate my life to working for economic and social equality in this society. Eventually, I would like to focus my practice on housing discrimination or education policy. For all of my misgivings about my obscure hometown, I have learned from living away from it that the ideal of community across socioeconomic lines, inevitable in a one-school town less than a mile square, has been diluted one subdivision at a time in most of America. It is my responsibility, and that of the entire next generation of social leaders, to remediate this corrosive separation. As a student, I have demonstrated a belief in the progress of both individuals and policy that will serve me well on my path to becoming a leader in this kind of community development.

Analysis

Despite the slight awkwardness of the first sentence, the starting paragraph does a good job of establishing an initial scene by using visual imagery to communicate Jordan Klimek's feeling of dislocation. Klimek does a particularly good of job of making his return stand out through original and vivid descriptions. The strongest aspect of the opening, however, is how it uses a common theme as the foundation of a strikingly original and deeply critical analysis of American inequality.

Many strong admissions essays leverage a single theme to illustrate something broader about the author. The particular genius of this essay is that Klimek opts for a topic, his experience as a small-town student teaching in an urban school that showcases his capacity for critical thinking while clearly demonstrating an intellectual passion that has inspired his previous experiences. At the same time, the story he tells looks forward, motivating his present interest in law school, and his future goals. He does an admirable job of demonstrating specific experiences that have created and supported that intellectual belief as well as placing these experiences in terms of his own personal development.

In fact, the times Klimek runs into trouble are the times when he departs from that compelling topic. He transitions to a brief explanation of internship experience, something that adds minimal substantive information beyond what a résumé could explain. That pushes aside his core themes of identity and growth to tack on an interest in public policy.

Klimek goes on to do a particularly admirable job with the concluding paragraph. Not only does he provide a strong explanation for how the theme of inequality would influence his legal education and future career, he addresses specific aspects of the law that he wants to address and how it would relate to his intellectual engagement. It also includes a unique segment of candor. His up-front denial of interest in practicing law only reinforces his actual reasons for law school. The result actually affirms a genuine intellectual interest that Klimek can pursue as a student. It provides a nice setup for an equally genuine and fervent conclusion that law school would provide him with a critical tool to pursue social action.

—*Raul Quintana*

MARISSA FLORIO

I am described as effortlessly astute, contagiously joyful, and cautiously spontaneous. I'm also boundlessly ambitious. It seems I am always undertaking a new endeavor, and my friends and family have slowly become desensitized in their reactions when I mention one day that I booked a flight on a whim to explore the sights of Madrid for a week alone, or that I began training to teach self-defense even though I had no prior experience, or that I gave up elevators for Lent when I lived on the seventh floor of my dorm building. When I joined both College Republicans and College Democrats, however, even my closest friends had to scratch their heads. Politics isn't necessarily a passion of mine, and they were confused as to who in her right mind would get involved in two organizations with such contrasting perspectives, members, and goals. Perhaps I'm not "of right mind": To me, it seemed like a perfectly logical thing to do. An important election was coming up, and while I had my own ideas and perspectives, I wanted to make sure I was exposed to all sides fully before I cast my first-ever presidential ballot.

I attended the two clubs' weekly meetings and soon befriended people in each. In both clubs, I was exposed to a combination of values I vehemently opposed and values I fully shared. I was surprised when, rather than opening my eyes to opposing ideas and changing my outlook as I had anticipated, my involvement in the clubs instead solidified my own previously held beliefs and values. I consider myself an open-minded person, but slowly I was narrowing my perspective rather than expanding it. I became more certain of my beliefs as I became more educated about them. This is one reason I see myself with a bright future in law. I am able and willing to see both sides of an argument and can respect diverse opinions, as I did at meetings, but I am also able to stand decisively in favor of one position over another.

This past spring, I worked for six months at the U.S. Attorney's Office (USAO) of Massachusetts as a part of my university's cooperative education (co-op) program. I went into the experience having always intended to go into law, but with the expectation that this internship would help me to narrow my focus and show me aspects of law I disliked. I wasn't sure if I would enjoy working in the government compared to a private firm. Perhaps prosecution wouldn't be for me. At the very least, maybe I would hate working with certain units within the office. A common refrain around my university's campus about co-op is that it oftentimes is most useful in showing you what you do *not* want to do. My time at the USAO did limit my career options, but not in the way that I had anticipated: I fell in love with the office and the passion of the people working there. I now will settle for nothing less than to become an Assistant U.S. Attorney myself someday.

Of all my different dimensions, my ambition and desire to continually stray outside my comfort zone are those that reap the most reward. If something sparks my interest, I invest myself fully and completely and always see it through to its culmination. From my freshman year in high school when I took a business law class designed by a local university, until this moment as I complete my law school admissions applications, I have always and will always continue to challenge myself and work toward my dreams. I'm thrilled to embark on the next leg of this journey toward achieving my aspirations, and would be honored for that journey to take place at Harvard Law School.

Analysis

Marissa Florio, despite unreservedly describing herself as "effortlessly astute, contagiously joyful, and cautiously spontaneous," manages to come across as exactly the sort of person you would want to handle your case in court. Although not explicitly included in her given list of epithets, her essay also illustrates her to be humbly aggressive and enthusiastically self-aware.

The danger lies with any application essay of painting with strokes too broad, and oversimplifying one's self. The résumé already gives broad strokes—there's no need to do so again.

Florio avoids repeating this by taking two episodes that might seem like the most typical application fodder to a critical eye, and allowing us to see the depth and complexity of experience lying beneath the otherwise unremarkable résumé lines.

Florio approaches the first experience with an opened mind

and leaves with a closed mind. Dual membership in the College Republicans and Democrats, which could have been evidence of childish naïveté, functions rather as proof of mature sensibilities. Florio appears to be less of a dilettante and more of an adult coming into her own, as she describes how the experience "solidified [her] own previously held beliefs and values."

The opposite mental transition happens with her second experience. Although she enters the Attorney's Office with the very college-like "expectation that this internship would help me to narrow my focus and show me aspects of law I disliked," Florio leaves it wanting to become an Assistant U.S. Attorney, a position that entails dealing with all aspects of the law.

Taken together, these experiences provide very convincing evidence that Florio is ready to enter professional life. She is not "open-minded" or "closed-minded," but changes between the two and is sometimes both simultaneously, which is what real life and the legal world demand.

Her example demonstrates the importance of knowing the image she projects throughout her application—after identifying how she appears at the outset, Florio is able to use the essay as an opportunity to provide the reader with a key to decode her résumé, and find within it a map of how her mind moves.

—*Nikhil R. Mulani*

ENUMALE AGADA

I was seven years old when I returned to Nigeria for the first time after my family's immigration to the United States. How do you describe returning to a place that you had always called home, but had never intimately known? A place that was deeply embedded in your being, but that was simultaneously so distant? I would describe it as pivotal. Reflecting upon that trip now, I realize that it was more of an awakening than a simple homecoming. It has taken years for me to identify the feeling that electrified me as soon as the plane landed. It was the same feeling that hit me as soon as I decided to pursue a legal career. It was the feeling of getting it right.

My status as an immigrant and its accompanying dual identities have always been intimately linked to my desire to pursue a legal career. Growing up as a Nigerian immigrant in America meant regularly existing in a liminal space between a world of privilege and innumerable opportunities on one hand and an equally proximal world of unimaginable limits and deficiencies on the other. In one world, I attended Stanford University, a renowned educational institution affiliated with one of the world's premier medical facilities while, in the other, I listened to my parents recount the painful story of losing their first child in Nigeria due to a lack of running water and basic medical equipment in their local city hospital. It was tensions like these that spurred my dedication to effecting social change and tackling the inequalities that exist in both of my worlds.

I plan to dedicate my legal career to public service and policy work with an emphasis on human rights and public health. I am not certain of what form this work will take, whether it be diplomacy, governmental legislation, or politics. What I am firm in, however, is my desire to pursue this path. My ambitions were cemented when I participated in a 2008 summer fellowship at the University of Cape Town's Gender, Health, and Justice Research Unit (GHJRU) as a medical anthropology student. During my time at the GHJRU, I worked with attorneys to shape South African health policy concerning rape victims and HIV-positive people based on research and interaction with these communities. It was here that I saw firsthand the power of the legal profession to impact the lives of people in a tangible way. The policy developed by the GHJRU ensured rape victims easier access to the potentially life-saving treatment post-exposure prophylaxis and demanded the ethical treatment of HIV-positive people by the South African Police Service. The GHJRU did not seek to speak for those for which it advocated—rather it sought to involve them in the discourse surrounding their health and their bodies by making them participants and stakeholders in the process. This was an invaluable lesson that I will forever carry with me and that will undoubtedly influence my own career.

Despite my experience at the GHJRU, I am not blind to the many inequalities and deficiencies that also exist in America. My volunteer work at the Black Coalition on AIDS (BCOA) in San Francisco, California, displayed the social issues that are realities in many American communities. With the BCOA, I worked to draft health policy for the city of San Francisco that was geared toward the physical, mental, and environmental aspects of health. An equally important aspect of this policy was its objective to make health care "intellectually accessible" to people with varying degrees of education, thus allowing all to be active participants in their own health care. This experience awakened me to the problems of underrepresentation and lack of proper access to resources that are all too often forgotten or diminished when placed in the American context. It also served as an important reminder of the fact that social issues such as these exist in all societies, even the most seemingly privileged and advanced.

As I prepare to add law student and, eventually, lawyer to my list of identities, I cannot help but reflect on the irony of my steadfast passion and single-minded ambition being borne out of the very tensions that I once viewed as an obstacle. However, I have and will continue to work relentlessly to reconcile these tensions within myself and in my surroundings. The biggest realization that I have made in my life thus far is that we do, indeed, have a voice in determining the people we become and the world in which we live. My greatest hope is that my work as a lawyer will be a lasting testament to this. With this in mind and armed with the unique perspective provided by the aforementioned experiences, I seek a legal education that will prepare me to not only shape health policy, but to reinvent the legal profession by taking a more holistic approach to policy development and legislation. For this reason, I respectfully submit my application to Harvard Law School for your consideration.

Analysis

This essay is about fusion. Enumale Agada's personal statement carefully fuses identity, experience, and commitment to his future goals. He skillfully harnesses a unique experience and hitches that personal story to his interest in enrolling in law school.

Agada first highlights the emotional tensions between living and learning in the United States and having roots in a third world country stricken by economic, social, and medical ills. This allows him to display his ability through cogent writing to explore nuanced issues. But Agada also gives himself a chance to showcase his own achievements when he explains how the tensions he describes led him to engage in certain academic and extracurricular pursuits that reflect his interest in public service and policy work. He does a fine job of highlighting his impressive résumé without focusing just on himself. Instead, he ties every activity to the positive impact the law can have on the world—he speaks not only of what he has accomplished, but also of what he has learned. Agada also smartly pulls away from his focus on the third world versus the first to explore how his interest in the law is applicable in America as well as overseas.

The essay ends with a strong conclusion that goes further than simply summing up what Agada has said so far. Agada recognizes how his essay could seem self-contradictory—noting that it is ironic that tensions many see as an obstacle have led to his drive and success—and then turns what could be perceived as a flaw into new insight. He hammers home the point that the circumstances into which he was born have not defined him and that he has the capacity to transform his own world. Then, yet again, he successfully draws a connection between this personal knowledge and his outlook on the law. And most importantly, he uses this connection to reveal his intent to use his distinctive perspective and knowledge of his ability to effect change to reshape the legal profession for the better. This bold final statement leaves the reader with a lasting impression of Agada's creativity, determination, and ambition.

—*Molly Roberts*

ISAAC HO

The institution of Evangelical Christianity serves many purposes: For some, it is a convenient farce, an expedient through which power, fame, and authority are acquired; for others, it is a source of moral guidance, a doctrinal foundation upon which ethics, ideology, and way of life are grounded; and for still others—for those whose faith constitute purpose itself—it is the very "bread of life." Growing up the son of Evangelical missionary parents, I was raised in a household for which the latter can be said.

Having served on several mission trips in East Asia, my parents brought my sister and me to the United States in 1994 as part of what *Time* magazine hailed as the "Whiz Kids" wave of East Asian American immigrants. In contrast to the vast majority of these highly affluent, economically driven migrants, my parents came seeking the opportunity to minister in various churches around the Southern California area. So while many of my Asian American peers grew up being taught the importance of academics, extracurriculars, and SAT scores, I grew up being taught the importance of prayer, worship, Bible study, and seeking first the Kingdom of God. In addition to being home-schooled and Christian-schooled nearly the entirety of my K-8 education, our family changed residences once every year or so in order to accommodate the transient nature of my parents' ministerial service. During this time, we relied heavily upon the financial contributions of those who believed in and supported my parents' ministries; my father often compared our circumstances to those of the prophet Elijah, who persevered in the ravine of Kerith because the Lord commanded ravens to bring him bread in the mornings. Through it all, faith remained at the center of our lives, overseeing and instructing everything from education to finances, from ideology to morality, from long-term outlook to everyday conduct. For my family and I, Christianity was truly—both literally and figuratively—the "bread of life."

Like so many who grew up within the church, my faith was

challenged in college. For the first time in my life, Christianity was not something that was spoken of in terms of "love," "hope," "faith," and "compassion," but more often than not in terms of "hate," "bigotry," "ignorance," and "intolerance." Though I initially thought that it was the world around me that had lost sense, the difficult realization hit during my second semester at USC that perhaps it was I who needed a broadening of perspectives. The more I sat in on lectures and engaged with others around me, the more I began to understand the context of my own faith and upbringing. Today, I remain proud to call myself a Christian, though one with a much broader worldview. I am ashamed of neither my faith nor my background, nor am I deluded about the role Evangelical Christianity has historically played in justifying the oppression of gays, lesbians, minorities, women, and practitioners of other faiths. Instead, I look eagerly toward the future, confident of our capacity for change and reconciliation.

What remains one of my greatest disappointments as a Christian and what I believe to be one of the greatest tragedies of sociopolitical discourse in the United States, is the antagonism that currently exists between members of the Religious Right and members of groups, which have historically been condemned by the Religious Right. In the New Testament, Christ states that He came to the world to love, not to judge; it was He who dined with the Samaritans and reached out to the outcast, it was He who wept with the widows and brought comfort to the downtrodden. This attitude of empathy and inclusiveness, regardless of ideology or social status, goes missing far too often in the discourse over issues like gay marriage, tolerance of other religions, women's right to choose, etc. Rarely do we hear from those who are willing to reach across the divide to offer voices of understanding and reconciliation. Having been raised from a uniquely spiritual background, my sincere hope is to use the legal education offered at Harvard Law School to put myself in a position where I can contribute to building a more empathetic society in which Evangelicals and non-Evangelicals come to a greater understanding of each other, to be able "to work together, to pray together, to struggle together, to go to jail together, to stand up for freedom together" as Martin Luther King Jr. so eloquently put it. Whether this ultimately means pursuing a career in private practice, public interest, academia, government, etc., I cannot profess to know at this point. What I do know is this is what I have my heart set on and am ready to dedicate my life to achieving.

Analysis

Isaac Ho's personal statement primarily focuses on his Evangelical Christian upbringing. One of the key strengths of the essay is Ho's candid style, which allows him to write expressively about the importance of his faith without becoming overly sentimental. Through the effective examples he chooses and his genuine voice, Ho makes it clear how for his family, "Christianity was truly—both literally and figuratively—the 'bread of life.'" He also establishes how he differs from the "Whiz Kids" stereotype applied to Asian Americans due to his humble upbringing, which asserts the uniqueness of his perspective early on in the statement.

The personal statement illustrates a clear chronological arc, beginning with how Ho's faith influenced his upbringing, how his faith was questioned in college, and ending with how changing his perspective on his faith inspired him to pursue the legal profession. Again, Ho's honesty serves the essay well when writing about his crisis of faith in college. He admits that he realized at college that he needed to broaden his perspective of his faith and describes how he learned more about the context of his faith and upbringing. Ho asserts that he can be proud of his faith while acknowledge the role of Evangelical Christianity in oppression. The complexity of this stance gives the statement a self-aware tone.

Though how Ho's faith and upbringing have influenced his decision to go into law is thoroughly substantiated, the essay may have been more effective if Ho mentioned any of his achievements in education or pursuits that relate to law. The bulk of the essay is a description of how he was raised and most of the specific details relate to his childhood or Bible quotes. How Ho's crisis of faith specifically inspired him to act would have made the personal statement more compelling. Additionally, Ho mentions that he wishes to attend Harvard Law School in order to foster a more empathetic society, but he does not specify why Harvard Law in particular would be a good fit for his needs.

Although Ho could have expounded more in those areas, he

does provide a personal window. Religion is not an easy topic to navigate in a few hundred words. Ho manages to provide an intimate, well-thought discussion that interweaves experience and ideas. That alone says a lot.

—*Hayley Cuccinello*

WHEN THE GOING GETS TOUGH

How we act in the face of adversity speaks to who we are as people. Adversity can take the form of a difficult upbringing, a painful decision, or the challenge of a job or internship. This brand of essay lets life's trials reveal true character. And the often-climactic tale of overcoming challenges works to make this genre a compelling read.

It's difficult to pinpoint exactly what constitutes a challenge. The examples of adversity that follow are wide-ranging, and many may even seem mundane, like the struggle to produce a presentation for an internship. But this type of essay isn't a race to produce the most daunting, horrifying set of experiences. The content of your obstacles matters—and a low course grade is a lot less damaging than a serious illness or personal loss—but the real goal is to explain how you dealt with adversity and what those actions show about who you are or who you became as a result.

If you have met challenging circumstances in a way that illustrates your character, by all means opt for an essay of this sort. And even though this category doesn't have the word "story" in it, you should still be telling a compelling one. Use vivid language, and take the reader along as you encounter challenges and overcome them.

CLAIRE M. HANKIN

I have always been determined to study subjects I am passionate about for the sake of the intellectual journey itself, rather than merely as a means to securing a place in the working world. That is why as an undergrad I decided to study philosophy and art, much to the dismay of my parents who had always pressured me toward the hard sciences. A desire to professionally combine my academic and creative interests had previously led me to pursue internships in entertainment law. Although I enjoyed the thrilling, fast-paced environment of working in the underbelly of popular culture, I was not completely satisfied and wanted philosophy to play a more significant role in my work.

Humanitarian law possessed the more direct link between theory and utility I desired. One goal of philosophy is to seek maxims of morality that can be understood across state and cultural lines, and at my current job our case work centers on globally acceptable behavior in the area of human rights. Moreover, my work at the firm frequently gives rise to debates that provide an opportunity for further application of my philosophical knowledge. These debates, inspired by current events or hypothetical situations, often go beyond the content of our case work and generate themes for op-eds or other writing projects.

When the recent conflict between Israel and the Gaza Strip prompted international attention and accusations of war crimes, my boss, Allan, a survivor of religious repression, felt compelled to say his piece. Unfortunately, the first draft I was given to review contained the same flaw as other articles I had read. It was a biased analysis with no reference to actual tenets of international law. How could anyone attempt to confirm or deny accountability for war crimes without discussing the law itself? Research and papers I had compiled for a class on "Just War Theory" during my senior year provided me with a plethora of resources and knowledge with which to supplement the article. It was easy for me to give merit to Allan's claims by finding relevant citations in primary sources of international law. The challenge was convincing him that his preconceptions were clouding his interpretation of the conflict. But after much deliberation and rewriting, we produced a coherent and more impartial analysis worthy of publication.

After "Proportionality and Disproportionality: A Guide to Arguments about Gaza" appeared in *The Huffington Post*, Allan was invited to a live discussion on the Arab news network Al Jazeera. I thought he did a great job of effectively communicating our argument; if you interpret the law to hold Israel accountable for war crimes, then you must acknowledge that Hamas is guilty of similar violations, if not more. But from my position off-camera, where I simultaneously watched the live broadcast, I could see what he could not. The once blue backdrop now featured a bold red title, "WAR ON GAZA," and image of the actual interview was replaced by a video of Israeli-imposed devastation and destruction. Instead of providing a credible counterargument, Al Jazeera, having already decided Israel was the aggressor, attempted to dilute our appeal to reason with a showcase of bloody circumstantial evidence.

The Al Jazeera interview, combined with the public's discomfort with the increasing disparity of civilian casualties, inspired us to expand our article to focus on the moral issues complicating the legal analysis of proportionality. Together we worked through the difficulty of assessing which values are to be measured against the loss of civilian lives. This time I was able to contribute even more of my theoretical knowledge as I helped Allan revise the article from a philosophical perspective he was unaccustomed to. For instance, I reminded him of the crucial distinction between *jus ad bellum* and *jus in bello*, ultimately providing a new structure for the article. "Gaza and Proportionality: When Do the Numbers Embarrass the Values?" was published in *Justice Magazine*, spring 2009.

The challenge of collaboratively writing this article taught me the importance of recognizing both the distinction and interaction between theory, law, and empirical context to avoid a politicization of the legal process that would inflame, rather than defuse, a conflict. It is thrilling to approach a challenge from multiple angles and I am proud to be able to use this skill to benefit the public by contributing to the publication of well-thought-out and reasoned articles. In addition to providing an invaluable foundation for my career, my time at AG International Law has given me the confidence that I can and will create my own niche in the legal industry, perhaps one that is new and innovative, where I can express my interests and talents. I want to be an advocate for justice, which requires an in-depth understanding of the values from which the law originates as well as its function within society. Having fully enjoyed my intellectual journey thus far, I eagerly await the new challenges I will face in law school and beyond.

Analysis

Claire Hankin's personal statement is effective because she not only elaborates on her passions (art and philosophy), but more importantly, she explains how these interests have been applied to her career and shaped her interest in law. It is extremely appealing for admissions officers to see that the candidate is simply studying what she loves, and that being a lawyer will simply further these passions. This essay does a great job expounding on the experiences that helped her discover and focus on the field of law that she wants to practice.

Hankin seizes the opportunity to show the admissions officer the genuine person behind all the listed credentials. Different accomplishments and publications are mentioned in one's résumé, but résumés do not explain the hardships or experiences behind these achievements. Hankin references her published articles, but more importantly, she demonstrates to the reader the obstacles that she faced when reviewing the articles. She also explains how her educational background assisted her in tackling these issues. Moreover, she connects how following her love of philosophy significantly helped her with her job—it allowed her to "approach a challenge from multiple angles." This essay is well-thought-out, for it shows the admissions officer her strengths as a lawyer, and that she will be a great asset to her classes and peers. She strongly indicates that her studies have made her distinctively qualified to work within her legal framework. The most salient aspect of Hankin's essay is that she showed that she is able to apply what she has learned in her education to her career. Furthermore, she states what she wishes to do with her career in law, indicating that she has a clear goal in mind and is sure of the direction that she is headed in.

—*Mariam H. Jalloul*

E.S.

Throughout my undergraduate education, extracurricular activities, and starting my own company, I have cultivated my passion for business. Simultaneously, I have also acquired a keen awareness of the interplay between our legal system and the business world.

I got my first taste for how important controls are in business as an intern in my university Office of Internal Auditing. Not long after the Patient Protection and Affordable Care Act (PPACA) was signed into law, I was assigned to draft a memo detailing how the law would impact operations at the university. As my university provides health insurance to most of its 16,000-plus employees, this was a daunting task.

Having just begun my internship, my project involved research on two fronts—university policies regarding health care, as well as PPACA provisions relevant to those policies. With this information, I was able to write a successful memo that helped the school's department heads organize the policy updates necessary to comply with the new laws. By the time the internship concluded at the end of that summer, I had been exposed, on a very large scale, to how the legal system and business world interact—something I would start to see in all of my future positions.

At the beginning of my junior year of college, a friend asked me to join a student-consulting group providing services to Israeli start-ups. Seeing a great opportunity to learn about how businesses are started, I accepted the offer and took a position leading a team of six other students. Our client was an online platform for anonymous communication. As we worked with the start-up to further develop the platform, we set about looking for ways to protect the company's intellectual property and found that a copyright would only protect the coding, or expression, of the platform, but not the idea itself. After extensive research, we decided the best way to supplement our copyright protection was to draw up nondisclosure and noncompete agreements for all employees and consultants.

Once we settled this issue, my team and I composed a business plan that gave the start-up a new marketing and development strategy and would help secure investor funding. Working with the start-up, and leading my own consulting team, I learned about every aspect, from legal to financial, that shaped the business. This gave me a unique viewpoint that has changed the way I look at all organizations, from start-ups to international corporations.

This past summer, I decided to put my experience from the consulting group and the start-up to use. While I spent my days working at a Big Four accounting firm, I dedicated nights and weekends to working with my brother to create a web-based marketing consulting start-up. Unable to pay a professional programmer to build the website, I decided to learn what I could about web design in order to build the site myself.

After setting up the site's basic foundation, I searched the Internet to find photos to use on our various web pages. As I explored, my uncle, a lawyer, mentioned that even pictures without a copyright notification could be copyright protected. He recommended that I make sure that all the photos I used were copyright-free. As it turned out, I had inadvertently selected many protected photographs and had to replace them immediately. The site is now complete and we have since begun alpha-stage testing.

Through experiences like these, I have had real-world, practical learning about the interdependencies between our legal and economic systems, and have become fascinated by how the two constantly evolve and shape one another. I aim to use my background working on the business side of these interactions to inform and support my study of their legal aspects. As a member of the legal community, this enhanced perspective will enable me to analyze each issue from both points of view and develop an understanding that draws on my experiences as a businessman and a lawyer.

I believe Harvard Law School would afford me a unique opportunity to continue my studies, particularly through its business law programs. One opportunity that especially interests me is the Transactional Law Clinics, where students offer legal aid to small businesses. Participating in these clinics will enable me to draw on my past experiences doing similar work, while also building my skills and knowledge through direct practice. A program like this would be a fitting and enriching element of my law school education, as well as my future legal career.

Analysis

Where many law school application essays are lacking, E.S.'s is quite successful: He explains in plain and convincing terms *why* he wants to attend law school. The admissions officer comes away with not only a clear understanding of the development of E.S.'s legal interest (at its intersection with business), but also an outline of how he'll use his law degree once he's earned it.

E.S. uses concrete examples from his experience on campus and in the field to illustrate his numerous interests and talents. E.S. proves that he is capable, effective, and excited for a challenge; he discusses drafting a health-care memo used by university officials, composing a marketing and development strategy for a start-up, and building his own company (while working a full-time job). E.S. manages to convey his many accomplishments without writing an essay that reads like a résumé. He also references, by name, a Harvard Law School program he'd like to become involved in. Though this might seem insignificant, it shows he's done his research (and is, perhaps, not just applying for "the name.")

E.S.'s interest in business and law seem certain; what's more ambiguous is who he is as an individual. His essay gives some indication of his character—the admissions officer gets the sense that he's both hardworking and curious. But E.S.'s essay might have benefited from an example of an experience or circumstance unrelated to his career—a discussion, perhaps, of a personal challenge he overcame. While it seems clear that E.S. will be a successful lawyer-businessman, the reader of his essay (who, remember, can grant only so many offers of admission) is left wondering who E.S. the *person* is.

—Lisa Mogilanski

RICHARD DAVIS

From the moment I first heard about No More Deaths, I wanted to support their work. No More Deaths was founded by an interfaith group of religious leaders from Tucson who were concerned about the fact that thousands of deaths were occurring along the U.S.–Mexico border as migrants traveling through the treacherous Sonoran Desert succumbed to thirst and heat exhaustion. In order to prevent these deaths, No More Deaths volunteers began patrolling migrant trails, providing food, water, and medical attention to individuals in need, and established semi-permanent water stations along these trails.

Growing up in El Paso, many of my closest friends as a child were Mexicans, or the children of Mexican immigrants. As such, I have always taken a deep personal interest in the immigration debate and in the plight of Latino immigrants. I was heartbroken about the tragedy occurring along the border, and felt compelled to try to help. But when I first had a chance to do so, during spring break of my sophomore year at Arizona State University, I almost let it pass me by. It was not that I had to choose between No More Deaths and another compelling opportunity. Rather, my choice was between embracing fear and overcoming it.

At that point in my life, I had not yet sought treatment for my anxiety disorder. This disorder first began to affect me early in my college years. One of the first panic attacks I remember occurred after a train I was taking from New York City to my girlfriend's hometown in New Hampshire hit and killed someone who was walking along the tracks. When the conductor announced over the loudspeaker that someone had been hit, I was overwhelmed with sadness and fear. I began to shake and hyperventilate; I felt intensely claustrophobic; I felt the need to run away, to escape the tragedy, to find a place of safety.

These sensations soon became all too common. Between the first panic attack and the panic attack that convinced me to finally seek treatment—which occurred in July 2010—I had over a dozen full-blown panic attacks, while less extreme periods of unexplained anxiety became almost a daily occurrence.

The night before I was to ride with the other volunteers to the No More Deaths campsite in southern Arizona, I had another panic attack. The emotions that filled me were intense. I was afraid of leaving the security of an American college campus, afraid to enter the uncertainty that I knew awaited me in the desert, afraid of the anti-immigrant vigilantes and the violent drug cartels that I knew were operating in southern Arizona. Most of all, I was afraid that I would be unable to cope with the suffering and sadness I might encounter. The volunteer training packet we had been given included instructions on what to do if we discovered a corpse. I was afraid that I wasn't psychologically stable enough to handle such a difficult environment.

Somehow, I went anyway. I didn't have an epiphany, a moment when my fear suddenly faded. I just gritted my teeth and forced myself to go, to do what I thought was right, in spite of the fear. And I ended up having one of the most rewarding experiences of my life.

Over the course of the week, I carried countless gallons of water and large quantities of food from our camp to various stations along the migrant trails. I didn't run into any anti-immigrant vigilantes or drug runners, but I did meet a father and his son from Chiapas, who were receiving medical treatment at our camp. Spending just a few minutes with this extraordinary pair was enough to dispel the stereotypes that many Americans have about migrants. They were polite, friendly, and very grateful for our assistance and for the chance to live and work in the United States. The son talked at length about how sad he was to have to leave his high school in Chiapas, and how he hoped to be able to continue his education as soon as possible. When asked why they decided to come to the United States, the father said that the economic situation in his community was simply too dismal to support his family. The son said he hoped to have his own chance at the American dream.

Franklin Delano Roosevelt's famous statement about fear is, of course, not literally true. There are many things that we ought to be afraid of: the prospect of nuclear terrorism, the evolution of antibiotic resistant bacteria, the effects of climate change. But FDR was right that our society must overcome the "nameless, unreasoning, unjustified terror which paralyzes needed efforts to convert retreat into advance" if we are to live up to the high-minded ideals that have defined the self-image of our nation since its inception. Just as it was necessary for me to overcome my fears of the border in order to be the person I wanted to be.

Analysis

This is a powerful essay that goes beyond the usual trope of overcoming adversity. All too often, application essays contrive stories of obstacles they had to circumnavigate in order to reach their current position. While this has become standard fare, it operates from the egocentric notion that there are not thousands of other applicants who have faced challenges of some nature at some point in their lives.

The potency of this essay is derived from the simple fact that its use of the tried-and-true "overcoming adversity" conceit is more than bromidic exploitation. This application truly tugs at the heartstrings of the readers, not because Richard Davis's story is any more compelling than his rivals, but because it is so personal. This story of conflict is not me-versus-the-world, but rather about the inner strength it takes to overcome the personal limitations. When reading this piece, the reader does not necessarily sympathize with Davis—instead, that commonplace emotional reaction is replaced with genuine empathy at the courage it took for him to end up where he is today, at a point to confront his own demons toward the goal of personal fulfillment.

The story of challenge overcome is not perfect. The nature of Davis's struggle comes across unclearly. It appears he has a serious medical issue. While the grin-and-bear-it, cold turkey approach he employs might be both brave and successful, it feels a bit simplistic—is avoiding a panic attack because Davis "gritted my teeth" or is it something more complex? Think carefully not merely about a challenge you've had, but also about how you overcame it, and what that shows.

That aside, in Davis's case, it helps matters that his success is manifested in such a way that it is used to assist others—specifically those for whom Davis deeply cared. Whereas many applications—both successful and otherwise—attempt to utilize sadness for their personal gain, this applicant takes that poignancy and turns it into an admirable tale of triumph over oneself and eventual amelioration of the lives of others.

—*John F. M. Kocsis*

TONY CARR

The pilot in me theorizes that ideally, my journey to the law would have occurred in a straight line at high velocity. But the aspiring lawyer in me comprehends the indispensability of the indirect path I've traveled. Upon graduation from high school amid the industrial decline of central Ohio in a family with no previous college graduates, higher education seemed out of reach, so I instead chose to enlist in the military. It was a fateful decision. The Air Force pushed me into direct engagement with a global and grand purpose, and taught me that continuous training of the mind was the key to success. This unleashed within me latent stores of ambition and intellectual curiosity, and I soon took on a sizable course load by night while working twelve-hour days, driven by the goal of becoming a pilot. Eleven years after taking the oath of enlistment, I flew one of the first aircraft to enter the airspace over Afghanistan in the wake of 9/11, delivering 34,000 humanitarian rations to Afghans displaced by the outbreak of conflict. Being presented with the Distinguished Flying Cross as a result of this mission was a profound experience that jarred me to inventory the larger purposes of my life and career. I developed a hunger to design and orchestrate operations rather than simply participating in them.

Over the next decade, I came to see wartime military service as the ultimate leadership university, a domain of constant learning and testing flush with the opportunity for growth. I've felt the weight of leading a fifty-one-aircraft formation executing the most complex airlift exercise since Vietnam. I've prepared the most senior officer in the U.S. military for his testimony to the 9/11 Commission, researching and investigating complex security issues and distilling them into messages for a global audience. I've had many such opportunities, but two novel experiences were particularly valuable in cognitively preparing to lead a large organization. In 2008 my graduate cohort visited Monte Cassino, a monastery in central Italy repeatedly ravaged by war throughout its 1,400-year existence. In a debate meant to explore morality in warfare, I was assigned to argue in favor of the abbey's WWII bombing. The following year, I published a thesis arguing that our coalition was taking an excessively physical approach to a social phenomenon in Afghanistan. These intellectual exercises involved the development of arguments using theory, logic, and evidence. Together, they provided a 360-degree perspective concerning a complicated issue of central public relevance. I found these experiences incredibly stimulating, and later, useful.

In 2010, I took command of an Air Force flying squadron, accepting total responsibility for 155 men and women operating aircraft valued at $2.4 billion. Attuned to the difficulty of service during protracted war, I focused not on marginal gains in operational outcomes, but on taking care of people. Through previous experiences, I'd become enlightened to the fact that if I fought for my people, they would fight for each other and our mission. They proved me right by surpassing every operational expectation and piling up countless accolades. While they did their jobs, I worked hard to safeguard their interests so they could stay focused and motivated. In one example, a subordinate was held liable for night-vision goggles stolen from his car. The amount of liability was equivalent to several months pay. Convinced the exorbitant fine was more concerned with deterring carelessness in others than creating fair accountability, I argued successfully that theft—not negligence—had been the proximate cause of the lost equipment, and his liability was sharply reduced. In another instance, an officer had her security clearance suspended when it was determined she'd sought counseling for alcohol abuse. Clearance adjudicators couldn't know that she'd developed a drinking problem while coping with an unresolved sexual assault, but had since recovered. I viewed the suspension as an unwitting re-victimization, and worked the system to restore her career. The job of commanding a squadron was rich with these opportunities, each masquerading as a nuisance in a profession with a laser-like focus on operational metrics. Each has reinforced within me the dawning realization that making a difference in the lives of individuals, immersed in the texture and nonlinearity attendant to dealing with people rather than machines, is how I'm meant to spend my energies. I'm drawn to the law because it celebrates difference making, rewards the pursuit of rightness, and requires activities I find most stimulating—research, argument, and intellectual combat for a purpose beyond the self. But those aren't the only reasons. I believe continued predominance of the rule of law depends upon leaders willing to dedicate themselves to its keeping, an activity to which I enthusiastically aspire. I'm hopeful my track record demonstrates my clear intent to bring dedication and diligence to the pursuit of public service, advocacy for those in need, and influence over how and under what conditions our Nation commits itself to war. I further hope you'll afford me the opportunity to begin navigating my next adventure at Harvard Law.

Analysis

Tony Carr skillfully weaves a unique and personal account of his indirect path toward law school in this successful application statement. Breaking free from the traditional constraints of the "I want to go to law school because . . ." essay, Carr effectively unites the pilot and the aspiring lawyer within him in a rich narrative, rife with colorful anecdotes.

Carr structures his essay as a journey that leads the reader though his decision to enlist in the Air Force, his development and leadership in the military, and the discovery of his passion for legal issues. From the start, Carr conveys a strong work ethic and effective management capacity without simply presenting a laundry list of accolades. From his experiences with debate and argument, admissions officers can get a clear sense of his intellectual curiosity and legitimate interest in advocacy.

The great strength of the essay may lie in the well-chosen and authentic examples of Carr's efforts to safeguard the interests of his squadron. He states his driving conviction that fighting for his people would allow them to "fight for each other and our mission." Without losing focus, he demonstrates how he effectively put to use an ability to skillfully interpret governing codes and a desire to champion fairness in the specific cases involving the theft of the night vision goggles and security clearance suspension. The gripping stories adeptly reinforce his own realization that he was meant to dedicate himself to "making a difference in the lives of individuals" through law.

The essay does possess a few long-winded phrases that could have been more effectively worded. Moreover, it draws upon some vague and nebulous concepts such as "difference making" that could have been more clearly expounded. But overall, this statement is a very effective personal reflection with a confident tone and a writing style filled with color and life. It offers a clear sense of Carr's passion for legal issues, the richness of his previous experiences, and ultimately his reasons for applying to law school.

—*Akua Abu*

MARA LUDMER

"Have you got what it takes to lead in a diverse world?" Based on these words, the Museum of Tolerance college internship program seemed like an incredible opportunity for me to learn about mentoring a coalition between Latino and Jewish high school students. A linguistic anthropology class I took at the time emphasized how language relates to socialization, miscommunication, and cultural differences. The program seemed to possess the potential to generate real change since it matched a theory discussed in my anthropology classes about a process termed "cultural evolution." This theory states that cultural change, whether positive or negative, starts by influencing the next generation when they are still impressionable and open to differences.

I jumped in with both feet. During my interview, the coordinator emphasized the similarities between Jewish and Latino students and explained the potential for powerful networks in the next generation. The program would start with a series of lectures by prominent community leaders and motivational speakers who would encourage team building between the two groups. My role would be to serve as a liaison between the groups and facilitate discussions each week. At the end of the year, the high school students would work in small groups to create a project that combined the two cultures and created an alliance based on similarity. I was absolutely thrilled to be offered the position.

Having grown up in a predominately white community, I picked UCLA partially because of the incredible diversity that both the campus and the city of Los Angeles had to offer. This was my first opportunity to really get involved in this diversity. The first day, I arrived at the museum ready for a new experience and excited to learn about the dynamic program that I felt could really draw a group of high school students out of their isolated bubbles.

As I glanced at the program syllabus and was introduced to the program directors, other mentors, and students, I wondered where the diversity had gone. Everyone in the room was Jewish. I wondered how we could build a coalition without the Latino side participating.

The answer was that we couldn't. Unfortunately, I learned that potential does not always translate into change. In reality, the Latino students were only involved in the program for three weeks (in a yearlong program). The rest of the time it was optional for them to attend and they received no incentive to come, whereas the Jewish students received school credit. Additionally, meetings were held at the museum, which was walking distance for the Jewish students and two hours in traffic for the Latino students. I understood why every single Latino student chose to forgo the program after the required time. This was the first time I watched a well-intentioned program with so much potential fail. The strangest part was that the directors of the program never acknowledged that it had not worked. Instead, they proclaimed it a success and considered running it again in the future. This angered me.

My anger was a catalyst in changing the program for my group. I spoke to the directors and the other frustrated interns about my concerns. I channeled my anger to lead my group of high school students to create a Jewish and Latino dance event hosted at UCLA. I felt satisfied that despite the flaws in the program we produced a final result that incorporated its original goals.

Although there was limited contact with the Latino students, I still met a variety of Jews. I grew up with the teachings of a Reform synagogue that my agnostic mother and father insisted I attend regularly. In contrast, the young people at the museum ranged in their religious beliefs from atheist to Orthodox. They also included Persians, Israelis, members of the LGBT community, and people of different socioeconomic backgrounds. Yet all of us congregated in the same room every week to discuss Judaism without the acknowledgment of the diversity that our own group represented.

This experience made me reconsider the difference between having the potential to make a change and actually accomplishing it. I still believe that cultural evolution or influencing the next generation can create great change in the way that people see others whom they immediately identify as different from themselves. I know that participating in this program was a starting point for me in recognizing the barriers I need to overcome when facing a diverse world.

The directors of this program were good people; they were amiable and passionate. But we can do better. I will do better. Like recognizing the flaws in this program, I hope to recognize the flaws in laws and work to improve them. Law school will give direction to my already developing passion for the environment. It will strengthen my power to make change in the world and, unlike the program directors, actually follow through. This follow-through includes the ability to acknowledge the inevitability of imperfection. I hope to help shape laws that create environmental reform and encourage sustainability, while boosting the U.S. economy. I am guaranteed to make mistakes, but law school will teach me to see the world through a different lens, challenging me to continue to analyze, reform, and improve every action I take.

Analysis

Perhaps one of the most common pitfalls in writing admissions essays is forgetting to talk about your own qualities. Too often do we see a well-versed and extremely well-written essay turned away simply because the author has focused on delineating the minute details of her story and has simply forgotten to elaborate on her own strengths and qualities. Here, however, we see an essay that moves the reader from the admirable vision, potential, and theory of the internship program, toward Mara Ludmer's outstanding contributions to the program. "My anger was a catalyst in changing the program for my group," is a great example of an effective transition into Ludmer's contributions to the program—she converts the evocation of a negative emotion, anger, into motivation and drive for social change within the program.

At certain points, however, the essay drifts into sounding like a résumé, from her core experience at the museum to creating a dance experience through it. It's important to remember that the personal statement exists to supplement and augment the rest of the application. A résumé can say, "Worked as liaison for Museum of Tolerance; led effort to increase diversity in program." Ludmer misses some opportunities to push past that. At a minimum, that résumé-listing wastes precious words in her brief statement.

Ludmer finishes off the essay by generalizing her experience from her time in the program into facets of everyday life, as well as her upcoming time in law school. This tie-in is extremely critical.

She recognizes her ability to apply the skills she garnered from her experiential learning to her career and education in law, making a connection that helps her stand out from the pool of applicants. Ludmer casts herself as intelligent but humble. She understands the "inevitability of imperfection" and admits, "I am guaranteed to make mistakes." Your essay shouldn't argue against your case for admission, but it should produce a real human being who can improve by attending law school, not one who stands nothing to gain from further study. Ludmer conveys an appreciation for the value law school can impart.

—Luke Chang

JUSTIN LU

As I stood in front of my class, ready to begin my first lesson, I felt a flash of déjà vu. I felt as though I had been there before, swimming in that sea of expectant gazes. In fact, I had spent a great deal of my life in front of audiences—I had been a debater all throughout high school, and I had spent the last three years of my life competing on the USC mock trial team. Audiences were no problem.

Painted on top of the sense of familiarity I felt, however, was a thin veneer of uncertainty. Audiences are no problem because you know that they only expect so much from you. They expect you to impress them. They expect you to win the argument with grace and aplomb. All my life, I had stood in front of audiences and put my best foot forward, and most of the time, that had been enough. As I paused to consider the forty pairs of eager eyes staring at me, however, I realized why I felt differently than I had ever felt in the past. I saw in those eyes a different set of expectations: a set of expectations that I had never had occasion to consider before.

As students, these people expected something different from me. They expected me to be a teacher. They expected me to engage with their problems in a meaningful way and to put my vanity aside in resolving them. They cared less about how I performed and more about how they performed. Standing in front of my class, with a staggering number of gazes fixed on me, I realized that it was time for me to step up.

Thankfully, I did. My first lesson was a resounding success. I found inventive ways to explain the abstract material we were dealing with, and my students seemed to respond. They raised their hands and asked insightful questions, all of which I answered with grace and with more than a little aplomb.

After I concluded class for the day, my reward came quickly and in quantities I could not have imagined. Students approached me in numbers and thanked me for teaching them something new. Competing on the intercollegiate mock trial circuit, I was used to being congratulated on a good performance, but I was less accustomed to being thanked for helping someone become better. As the weeks wore on, I began to feel more accomplished than I had ever felt before. My students were improving, and the feeling was indescribable. My focus rapidly shifted from my own performance to the performance of my students.

I realized, somewhat later, that this sense of accomplishment was exactly what I had always been looking for in life. Helping real people with real problems gave me a stronger sense of purpose than public speaking for its own sake ever had. Helping people that I cared about improve themselves gave me a greater sense of joy than winning an award for excellence ever could.

Still, I was careful to let my emotions be tempered by an abiding sense of personal responsibility. More than ever before, I could see the effect that my words had on people. For better or for worse, I was uniquely positioned to influence my students' manner of thinking. They relied on me, not only to tell them what to do, but to show them how to think as well. For some students, that meant taking more time to explain difficult concepts; for others, that meant persuading them to take a more active interest in their skills and in their futures.

I realized then that I had to be more than just a teacher—I had to be an advocate, too. I advocated on behalf of my students' goals and abilities, and I advocated against their own laziness and self-doubt. This task demanded patience and flexibility from us all, but by the end, everyone had gained a better understanding of a singularly important aspect of their future—including me.

I had always known that I wanted to be a lawyer, and now I finally knew why. I knew that I wanted to spend my life in the service of ideas, and I wanted to do so on a grander scale than a single classroom could provide. Among the many roles a lawyer must play in our society is that of a teacher. Lawyers inform, persuade, and trade on the power of their ideas. All my life, I had tried to prepare myself to take on this role, and now I finally had the necessary experience and perspective to embrace it fully.

As I stood in front of my class, ready to begin my final lesson, I felt a flash of déjà vu. I felt as though I had been there before, only this time, I felt at home. I stood in front of my students and began my lesson, confident that I could help them learn something new. After all, I had already spent more than a hundred hours in front of them doing exactly that. Students were no problem.

Analysis

Justin Lu's perceptive and subtle account of the relationship between performance and service in the legal profession makes this essay sharp and original. In particular, Lu effectively uses the transition from debating to teaching to underscore a crucial shift in his measure of success; while debating defines success in terms of personal performance, success in teaching depends on the pupil's achievement. Emphasizing the greater fulfillment that comes from the latter measure of accomplishment, Lu transitions from his personal experience to his ambition to become a lawyer, showing maturity and a deep sense of awareness of the moral implications of his prospective career.

After a concise opening that introduces the experience of facing an audience as the unifying theme of the essay, Lu slowly reveals the significance of this specific experience piece by piece, building up interest and expectation on the part of the reader. This personal narrative reaches its climax only in the sixth paragraph, where using a simple yet powerful epiphany Lu points to the "stronger sense of purpose" and "greater sense of joy" that came from teaching. The conclusion gives the essay an elegant circular structure by recalling the same moment recounted in the introduction—Lu standing in front of his class—and by repeating a different version of the very last sentence of the opening paragraph—"Students were no problem."

Although the connection between the skills required in teaching and those required in the legal profession is not particularly immediate and may seem far-fetched, the depth and persuasiveness of Lu's motivation to become a lawyer outweighs the arguably forced link. Similarly, Lu's strong and distinct voice makes up for a narrative that sometimes lacks the descriptive vividness that would enhance the reader's empathy with the author.

—*Francesca Annicchiarico*

NATALIE RAD

The Iranian government operative I sat across from was clearly growing weary of being interviewed by me, a woman at least forty years his junior, and from the minority group he spent his life discriminating against. "I am well aware that the Jews [in Iran] live a double life—in the streets a man says his name is 'Mousa,' but at home his family calls him 'Moshe.'" His statement caused me to tremble. Was his statement an honest reflection or a subtle threat? This man was one of the Islamic revolutionaries who helped bring Ayatollah Khomeini into power during the Islamic Revolution of 1979 in Iran, the revolution that changed the course of my family's history, and the lives of countless other Iranian Jews. This interview, along with a series of others I conducted throughout Iran, was part of the comprehensive research I did before writing my book, *A New Cold War*, about political relations between the United States and Iran and Iran's political and legislative history. Following a series of tragedies that befell my family at the hands of the Iranian government, I researched and wrote a book to understand the precarious state of affairs in a nation that for centuries was my family's home. In the process, I discovered my calling as an attorney, serving as an advocate for the voiceless.

In the summer of 2003, my grandfather was killed in Iran because of his Jewish identity. Ultimately, his legal system failed to protect him from religious discrimination of the most serious degree. I soon discovered that this was not the first time my family was the target of intolerance. My great-uncle, my grandfather's brother, was publicly executed during the Islamic Revolution in 1979 because he was a wealthy Jew and the revolutionary government wished to seize his holdings. Even though the loss of my grandfather weighed on me greatly, the end of his life served as the catalyst for my exploration of the fields of public policy and law. I set out to find an explanation for the current state of affairs in Iran through learning about the religious codes that penetrated its legal framework. I soon broadened the scope of my research to other Middle Eastern states and found similar trends in the evolution of their governments and laws, leading me to go back through history to examine their origins. For the next four years, I continued to research the laws and legal systems of many Middle Eastern states as well as the development of their political relations with the United States. After years of research, interviews, and broad discovery, I channeled my findings into a book.

When my book was ready for print, I excitedly phoned my family in Tehran to tell them the great news. I received a reaction I was unprepared for, but should have anticipated: fear. My family urged me to publish under a pen name and remove any mention of my grandfather's life because they were terrified of retaliation. The regime that had killed my great-uncle and my grandfather was now silencing me. In that moment, I realized that although a book can serve as a platform for shedding light on information, it can only go so far when it comes to initiating real change. My decision to refrain from publishing my book demonstrates how fear of government retaliation can create self-censorship. The one thing that can combat this fear and protect an open forum for self-expression is the law. The U.S. legal system's protection of the right to free speech is not something I take lightly. My deep appreciation for U.S. constitutional law is born of its ability to allow individuals to openly express their ideas without the fear of persecution.

Equally important is the law's ability to reconcile differences between conflicting parties and ensure justice is served. A book is one outlet for voicing the need and means for a change in public policy, but actual improvements to the legal framework are only achieved through the enactment of laws. While a book can explore a set of facts in conjunction with differing opinions, the law is an essential tool that uniformly addresses the merits of each view and links conflicting interests, however diverse each may be. Lawyers can be the agents for change by linking the concerns of minorities to the constitution's protection of an individual's inalienable rights. I am eager to study and influence the legislative texts that shape our lives, thereby giving a voice to those who suffer from discrimination. Thurgood Marshall's career is an exemplary case of a lawyer's ability to use the legal system to secure the interests of a minority group. Hopefully with time and effort, the threat to my family in Iran will subside and the opportunity to publish my book will emerge once again. By pursuing a law degree and ultimately working as constitutional attorney, I will empower myself to contribute to the legal protection of minorities, thereby honoring the loved ones I have lost.

Analysis

While the events detailed in this essay are compelling in their own right, it's the cohesion of this essay's narration that separates it from others. Natalie Rad starts in a relatively safe manner—placing the reader "in the moment" of a particularly stressful episode, but then goes beyond that moment to reveal a broader life path that exquisitely justifies her interest in the law. The interview described in the first paragraph would be meaningless without the context of Rad's life, and it is her depiction of that life that both adds meaning and entices the reader to consider her as a worthy applicant.

Had Rad started out with the last paragraph, assaulting the reader with an abstract claim about "the law's ability to reconcile differences," there's no doubt that this essay would have been passed over as yet another try-hard attempt to display familiarity and interest in the law. What Rad does instead is recognize the fact that the most important and interesting part of an application is not that the person who filled it out is interested in law (that's already apparent), but *why* that person is interested in law, and what events in her life have driven her to this conclusion. A personal statement is supposed to say something personal, intimate perhaps, that allows the reader to begin the process of understanding the writer's motivation for writing, and this essay accomplishes that goal convincingly. The abstract statements of the last paragraph flow from the narrative established in the first three; it's only after Rad has established her personal journey that she deals with its logical conclusion: going to law school.

At the same time, this essay, while successful, isn't perfect. Rad's decision to leap from details about having to censor her own writing to meditating on the ultimate value of the printed word strains the credulity of the reader and invites the criticism of forcing her rationale for law school into a place where it doesn't belong. Still, the collective force of Rad's narrative manages to quiet the reader's unease, ultimately making for a successful essay.

—*John Finnegan*

DASHA WISE

The large room was beginning to feel like a cramped interrogation chamber as we stood anxiously awaiting the next set of difficult questions. We did not have to wait long. Why were there discrepancies in our numbers? Wasn't the retreat expense unnecessarily large? Not to mention that the submitted documents were not only late but incomplete! I could not help but steal a glance at the outgoing treasurer standing next to me—as a newly elected executive board treasurer for Community Impact (CI), Columbia's largest service organization, I had been invited to accompany her to CI's annual presentation to request funding from the student councils. There was no doubt that she had stayed up most of the night completing this presentation, attempting to patch up holes in the financial records. I could not blame her for the mistakes—everyone at CI was overworked and stretched well beyond their capacity, too busy keeping up with the activities of each day to step back and tackle the organization's underlying problems.

As she became visibly more flustered, I knew that I needed to assume responsibility for the remainder of the presentation. Standing there in defense of the organization that I had come to love, I managed to remain calm, fielding critical questions to the best of my ability while swallowing the all-too-well-founded criticism along with my pride. As the presentation came to a close I began to understand the systematic change that was necessary, and that I would be responsible for making this change a reality.

I began immediately that summer. Learning as much as possible about the current system and its flaws enabled me to discover that CI's largest impediments were operational inefficiency and improper communication, the combination of which was contributing to internal frustration, ineffective resource management, and a tainted reputation. To establish both fiscal accuracy and efficiency I reconstructed treasury procedures and devised an automated budget-tracking and request processing mechanism that would be administered through CI's online platform. Working closely with our webmaster, I designed a treasury section for CI's website that would enable coordinators to request funding, monitor their budgets, and access key forms as well as the instructional manuals that I had written over the summer. To reposition CI's public image, I insisted on transparency, persuading the staff of its importance and holding a board meeting to update important documents such as our constitution and spending guidelines. Reflecting CI's core principles and procedures, they would now be publicly displayed on our website.

In pushing for large-scale change I knew in advance that overseeing the process would be no easy task and that I would need to hold numerous trainings, respond immediately to student inquiries, and continue to work throughout the year to make further corrections based on feedback and my own observations. All this I was prepared for, and with input from my peers and CI's staff along the way, I arrived at a product that would provide the CI treasury with structural support for years to come. CI's records were finally accurate and we were able to cut costs, monitor our spending, and receive approval from our volunteers, for whom the elusive red tape had now given way to simplicity and predictability. A system that responded to the needs of students, board members, and staff alike eliminated needless frustration, established procedural efficiency, and improved both internal and external communication.

When I found myself in front of the student councils exactly one year later I was not met with the same mistrust and quizzical expressions. Our presentation, whose supporting documents had this time been submitted well in advance and verified multiple times, resulted in open gratitude for the effort that we had put in to establish fiscal accuracy and procedural transparency and to maintain open communication with the councils, informing them of the changes that we were making in light of their concerns. Unlike the previous year's penalty and subsequent funding shortage, this time we received precisely what we requested. Yet perhaps most importantly, we received respect, not only from our own coordinators, volunteers, and other constituents, but from the university as a whole.

Although I had encountered numerous difficulties throughout my life, what I had decided to tackle at CI last year was my most significant challenge yet—not merely for the amount of effort that it required, but for the fact that my decisions now affected, whether directly or indirectly, hundreds of others, from CI's staff and student executives to our nine hundred volunteers and the nine thousand individuals that they served. In some quantifiable sense, this was my largest accomplishment, the most rewarding and among the most memorable, but it was not the first and it will not be the last. I would not have it any other way. For to survive difficulties is one thing, but to excel *in spite* of them is another. Overcoming the most seemingly insurmountable yet worthy challenges is, for me, the primary means of obtaining respect from the one person that truly matters and is at the same time the most difficult to please— myself.

Analysis

Dasha Wise's essay manages to convey not only her personal qualities that would make her a good lawyer but how she was able to harness these character traits in the face of adversity. She starts out with a compelling hook, setting the scene with a description of the interrogation-esque defense of her service organization's budget she was faced with as a newly minted treasurer. While also highlighting her involvement with an organization and a position that are helpful training for lawyers-to-be, she also opens up the opportunity to show the admissions officers how she deals with difficult situations.

Wise continues by demonstrating her ability to step up and fill leadership positions as well as her passion for the organization she is involved in. Through the narrative, she relays her tenacity and her willingness to delve to the bottom of the problem, do her research, and address the root of the issue, rather than attempt to treat only the symptoms of the problem. Furthermore, Wise makes apparent her ability to address all facets of the problem, at once exemplifying her holistic view of the problem as well as the way in which she works with others to enact the change she has determined needs to be made. All of her hard work comes together at the end of the narrative, where, at the next year's review, the effects of her labors of the last year are very clear.

Wise does make some grandiose statements, but for the most part she supports and enriches all the character traits she wants to convey to the admissions board with a real-life example that also serves as the backbone of her essay.

When writing about a challenge you've faced, try to pick an

example that shows off many different sides of your personality. Wise picked an example where she could not only describe her role as a leader but also her ability to put in hard work and enact real change in something she is passionate about.

Wise may have wanted to include some statements about why she wants to be a lawyer in this essay, and connecting her desire to go to law school with the passion she had for bettering her organization is one path she may have wanted to consider. However, her narrative about her time as treasurer for Columbia's Community Impact served as an excellent vehicle for conveying the character traits that would make her a prime candidate for Harvard Law School.

—*Layla Siraj*

THINKING CRITICALLY

Law schools are looking for students who will think carefully and critically every day. Few actions demonstrate your ability to reason and think as do actual reasoning and thinking. Many essays wrestle with important questions of ethics and policy, showcasing a depth of thought, as well as a sophisticated concern for the sorts of issues applicants will face as future lawyers.

The "thinking" essay comes with its share of potential stumbling blocks. An overly didactic and distant tone can spoil any essay, but it can especially hurt one that relies on more abstract thought and reasoning. An excess of droning abstraction can easily spill over into ramble. To avoid that hazard, many of the essays in this section mix their deeper, more reflective portions with experiences and discussion of identity. Life abroad in Madagascar informs a consideration of democratic values; reflection on identity intertwines with reflection on the Israeli-Palestinian conflict; a pair of internships generate thoughts on the intersection of criminal justice and statistics.

In the right dose, this type of essay can offer a window into your mind that a raw LSAT score might not. Of course, all personal statements demand a heavy element of critical thinking. But don't be afraid to add the more cerebral interpretations and extensions of your stories and experiences. After all, it's law school you're applying to.

OSCAR STANTON

It wasn't until Mihaja turned off the television that I realized I could still hear gunshots in the distance. It was the first weekend of my semester abroad in the capital city of Antananarivo, Madagascar, and the deadliest day to date of the political crisis that began just before I arrived. I sat on the living room floor as my host parents ushered five-year-old Aina and ten-year-old Mialy into another room, troubled by having exposed them to the gruesome images on the news. Over the following months, I traveled around the country, pursuing my goal of learning about Malagasy culture, and constantly hearing news and opinions about the political situation. The more I learned, the more unstable my understanding of democracy became.

I arrived in Madagascar directly after an eventful and life-changing election season in America. As a delegate at the Democratic National Convention, I had experienced firsthand the level of involvement ordinary Americans can have in the electoral process. The election had defined my fall semester at Bowdoin, and the smooth transition of power on January 20 felt like the victorious end to a battle that I had helped fight. The volatile situation I was thrown into in Madagascar a few days later looked and felt nothing like my American model of democracy, although technically Madagascar is a democratic republic. Many Malagasy citizens felt that past President Ravalomanana took advantage of the people for his own economic gain. But I didn't sense the same fervent support for Rajoelina, the opposition leader, which I had felt for Barack Obama in 2008. My host mother, for example, seemed concerned with the violence but surprisingly disinterested in the social and political debate. She dismissed the protestors as *"profiteurs,"* merely taking advantage of an unstable situation to riot and loot as opposed to fighting for meaningful social change.

I had, and still have, a hard time making sense of the picture of democracy I saw failing in Madagascar. Perhaps democracy isn't as fail-safe as I had imagined in the convention center in Denver, or in the voting booth on November 4. The United States has proved that democracy can work very well in a certain context, but does it necessarily have the same potential in other contexts? The fact that democracy might not be a universal concept, as I once unthinkingly accepted, led me to question the universality of many of my other beliefs.

Through the honors project I am embarking on this fall, I am discovering that my previously static view of the universality of human rights is, like democracy, much more complicated in reality. I have always been conscious of the concept of human rights; from values instilled in me during childhood to my two-summer internship at an LGBT rights organization, it has become an integral part of my life to recognize injustice and follow my passion to eradicate it. My first summer at Family Equality Council introduced me to human rights work in the United States, and my interest in anthropology led me to explore the pursuit of human rights in other societal contexts. As I studied cultural difference, I learned how life experiences differ across societies, and how women's roles, statuses, and hardships differ with them. The nonjudgmental relativism with which many anthropologists aspire to view other cultures can often clash with lawyers' and policy makers' ideas of fundamental rights. My honors project examines the intersection of anthropological and legal debate in women's rights initiatives around the world. I am particularly interested to learn how legal decisions in the United States and Europe treat cultural differences when they address women's rights. I believe that anthropology and ethnography have an incredible capacity to inform lawyers and policy makers, enabling them to bring about culturally logical and progressive change.

What I have learned over the past several years about culture, democracy, and human rights has led to me to many questions and few answers. I am still grappling with these complex concepts, and I look forward to examining them from new perspectives as a law student and lawyer.

Analysis

Immediately, the reader is pulled into this essay with the perilous image of a country torn by civil war in the midst of a political transition. This is something you want to aim for in your own essay. You don't have to paint a picture of a battle scene in order to grasp the attention of the reader, but be very selective and purposeful in the image you try to create. Pick something that will make any person want to continue reading. What makes the rest of this essay successful is that Oscar Stanton is able to weave two important passions into one cohesive narrative. He speaks of his time in Madagascar and how he juxtaposed that political experience to the one he had in the United States just days before. He lets us know that he played a part in the 2008 campaign but makes his experience seem far more significant by coupling it with other experiences he has had. He then transitions into his most recent project, which demonstrates another side of his interests with ease.

Most impressively, Stanton is able to demonstrate a complex understanding of his world and the many issues that are intertwined. He isn't just listing his accomplishments and accolades, but incorporating them into a greater narrative. This is an incredible quality that you should always try to implement in your essay. Stanton acknowledges that his accomplishments are more than just singular entities but, rather, in combination have given him the tools that may make him a worthy candidate for Harvard Law School. Ultimately, to make your personal statement stand out you should aim to pay attention to the details that you incorporate, use your experiences to create a cohesive narrative, and incorporate your understanding of how your experiences will allow you to have a larger impact on your future endeavors.

—*Mandi Nyambi*

MICHAEL ELIAS SHAMMAS

My heart dropped; my world collapsed. Barely discernable beyond the swirling dust and debris, a doll-sized child lay sprawled on the charred ground. She held a bloodstained Mickey Mouse toy in one of her delicate hands, looking at first glance as if she were asleep, as if her mother—who lay motionless just a few feet away—had comforted her before the longest sleep of all. The knob in my throat tightened. I thought: "Who will bring the dead justice?" The answer came fast, too easily: No one.

I sighed. The girl's father fell to the ground, clutching what remained of his daughter—just a distended pulp of flesh and bone—and weeping. His tears pocketed the dust like little bombs, erupting particles of sand into the air, dissipating the puddle of blood. His expression at that moment—lines gone, face blank in stark recognition of his loss—could not have been more peaceful. Yet then he stood, slowly and wearily, and gazed at the camera before swearing an appalling oath to avenge his loved ones even if it meant "wiping out the enemy," even if it meant tearing holes through their lives as large as the ones the Israeli bombs had torn through his.

I turned away from the television and gazed at the floor. "This is why these conflicts will never end," I whispered, thinking of the man's horrifying words. At the moment I knew nothing to be truer than this thought, nor crueler. I looked out the living room window and took in the scene: cars, bicycles, basketballs, dogs, a barbecue, a couple holding hands and walking, all highlighted by a brilliant American sun. I thought: "There are such different realities in this small world of ours. Such needless tragedies."

In a much lesser way than the family above, my immediate family members were also casualties of the 2006 Israel-Hezbollah war. I remember my mother's tears and my father's anxiety as they watched their childhood villages in Lebanon transform into war zones. I remember the cognitive dissonance that came from both empathizing with Israel in its battle against Hezbollah and despairing of the deaths of Lebanese and Israeli civilians. I remember arguing fervently with a Hezbollah supporter, wondering whether he would be willing to destroy his own country in the macabre hope that he could destroy another.

Throughout my life, this pattern repeated itself after every bombing or assassination. I am sorry to say that, as a result, I often felt embarrassed at school and ashamed of my heritage. Why couldn't they stop fighting? Was something inherently wrong with the Lebanese? During my summers in Lebanon I would sometimes stare at the surroundings—the glistening Mediterranean and the Roman ruins and the Crusader forts dotting the hilltops and the mosques standing next to the churches. I would see the faces of children who—Druze or Sunni, Shi'a or Christian—were undeniably beautiful. At such moments, my questions would grow more perplexing. What could motivate one to destroy such beauty?

My heritage posed the above question, and it has repeatedly provided the answer: passion. A month ago, minutes into a dinner gathering of my parents and their Lebanese friends, the topic turned (as usual) to politics. Soon a peaceful conversation between perfectly rational people escalated into a shouting match over who was right in the Syrian conflict. The fifteen-year civil war my parents escaped was brought up, blame tossed about, and I felt a sense of dismay as—gazing at a pulsing vein on my father's forehead—I realized the inevitable: There will, very probably, be another war. We Lebanese care too much about our differences for anything else. Worse, our passion blinds us to reason.

Hotheaded passion killed so many Lebanese and Israelis in 2006, and hotheaded passion will continue to kill. This does not have to be the case. My best friends are Jewish. A favorite professor is Muslim. I myself am Eastern Orthodox Christian. We get along extremely well, and I often wonder how to transport this peace to the Middle East. Because the passion is here to stay, because the bitterness is so strong, I believe international law is the only answer; by delegitimizing murder, it can act as a dam against the terrible flow of hatred. My life's task as a lawyer will be to plug the many holes in this dam.

There was a time when I thought that if only others could see that little girl sprawled on the ground, Mickey Mouse in hand, the fighting would stop. But I know better now. The worst elements of human nature are universal, and these elements yield a passion that is strong enough even to kill little girls. This passion gains legitimacy from five-word slogans and shiny uniforms and dogmatic ideologies. This legitimacy can be undermined by new norms, and these norms can be perpetuated through a stronger system of international law. There is a gap between what international law does and what international law can do. The misery in the Middle East is a large part of what triggered my interest in law, of what inspired me to take my first international law course in high school and to study international relations, and I hope it will help show me ways to close this gap. The lives of so many people depend on its closure.

Analysis

Two things stand out about this essay. The first, and probably most intriguing part of the essay, comes right at the beginning, though not in the way you'd expect. The vivid descriptions present in the first paragraph convince the reader that Michael Shammas is drawing from his own experience to present this scene to you, but the second paragraph reveals the camera acting as a proxy, with the scene he's describing actually taking place far away, leaving him totally removed from the gory action he describes. This turns the usual expectation of personal statements on their head—the scene is not personal, Shammas is not confronting these horrors directly. He's instead observing them from the comfort of his own room. It's a risky move, because it can easily come off as inauthentic and cheap, but in my opinion Shammas manages to walk the fine line between art and the artificial.

A strong use of language helps that achievement. The image of "the little girl sprawled on the ground, Mickey Mouse in hand" evokes feeling; Shammas isn't an eyewitness, but these realities are dear and close to him all the same. In another technique, Shammas intersperses concise, terse sentences throughout the essay. The dense punch from lines like, "This does not have to be the case," further conveys a sense of feeling.

The second thing that stands out is that, after the opening, Shammas manages to logically justify his desire to enter into international law in a manner that comes off as both reasonable and justified. By interweaving his personal experience into the rest of the essay, Shammas turns from the subversion in the first two paragraphs to an honest opening of his life to the reader, detailing the ways that the conflicts in the Middle East have affected him, even though those ways aren't as visceral as the first experience he described. Shammas intimately ties his own life to the area he wishes to study, inviting the reader to believe his claim of wanting to end "[t]he misery in the Middle East," and providing reasons that can resonate with the reader, since like him, very few law school admissions officers have ever actually been exposed to the horrors of war directly.

Shammas takes on a thorny issue with a score of potential pit-falls. Yet he manages, by dint of critical thinking and analysis, to illustrate his rigor of thought. He does that while connecting the topic to his personal motivation to study international law, and to do his part in seeking solutions.

—John Finnegan

RITU GUPTA

With latex-covered hands and goggled eyes, I maneuvered the flask in my palm, scrutinizing it for a trace of my chemical product. Recalling the hundreds of grams of alkaline salts I had fused as the initial reaction in this sequence, my coresearcher and I marveled at the milligram of product that remained after two years. We had, at last, successfully synthesized our target molecule, the potential drug candidate, Napyradiomycin A1 (NAP A1).

My interest in law burgeoned from the seeds of scientific inquiry. As a graduate researcher, I complied with federal and university regulations that governed issues of chemical storage and waste disposal. Importantly, laws also determined the practical fate of innovations: that is, whether students could claim ownership of their intellectual property. When formulating the synthesis of NAP A1, my research team and I emphasized atom-economy and environmental sustainability while developing a chlorination process that overcame a significant chemical hurdle. Together, these features made our synthesis desirable, and thus potentially patentable.

My fascination with the intellectual property issues governing my synthesis exposed me to the intimate relationship between science and law that prevailed even outside the laboratory. From the inception of an idea to the ownership of a chemical product, science is governed by the boundaries of law. Nevertheless, this dependence is constantly evolving. When complex, multidisciplinary scientific problems raise legal and ethical questions that fall outside the scope of existing laws, scientists unwittingly initiate the development of novel intellectual property laws, or the modification of existing ones. In this context, cooperation between those who speak the language of science and those who understand its relevant laws becomes a critical feature for both scientific and legal progress. Already fluent in the language of science, attending law school will enable me to understand the language of laws. With bilingual fluency, I want to harness the synergy of my dual backgrounds toward their mutual progression.

One instance in which scientific progress has raised ethical questions that require legal remedies is illustrated in the ongoing crisis between pharmaceutical companies and the people of developing countries, who are often unable to afford the patent-induced prices that such companies charge for their drugs. Local drug manufacturers are then induced to infringe patents and instead manufacture generics. As a scientific investigator-cum-lawyer, I value the patent system that internationally rewards innovation, and want to contribute to remedies such as drug credit schemes to ensure that equitable access to vital medicines precludes patent infringement.

As a nascent student of law, I am excited to employ the analytical and writing skills I have acquired as a chemist toward the solution of legal problems. Just as organic chemists rely upon prior methodologies and published reactions to provide a framework for product formation, lawyers rely upon precedent. No two chemical problems are identical, however, and thus adaptation is critical. In the same way, legal problems arise from a variety of issues that necessarily differ from one case to another. Already harboring an analytical framework for legal problem solving that will enable me to navigate complex cases, the writing skills I have acquired vis-à-vis involvement in our research group's journal submissions will further bolster my command of intellectual property law, which necessarily demands technical writing.

In our ever-more interdisciplinary world, scientific innovations and laws inform and influence each other, ultimately emerging in response to each other. I wish to integrate my scientific domain knowledge, garnered through my undergraduate years and fortified as a graduate researcher working on the synthesis of NAP A1, with my emerging legal skills, through my role as an intellectual property lawyer. Thus harnessing the synergy of these fields, I want to ensure that our lawful society reaps the benefits of its scientific engine.

Analysis

Ritu Gupta's beginning anecdote sets the stage for what is a very successful essay. Gupta already distinguishes herself in these opening lines by describing a scene from her days as a graduate school researcher in chemistry. This anecdote not only qualifies her knowledge of chemistry but it also provides a snapshot of her life that is unique and more likely to be remembered by the admissions officer reading her essay.

After beginning with a scene, Gupta does a great job of connecting her science background to her newfound passion for the law. She paints an image of herself doing research in the lab, developing the new synthesis for NAP A1 but then discovering all of the legal issues surrounding the intellectual ownership over this property. This second anecdote follows smoothly from the first, and it is effective at describing how questions of patent law continued to arise for her both inside and outside the laboratory.

Gupta's essay is also successful because it specifically communicates why she is applying to law school. Her passion for science is already well established in the beginning of the essay, and Gupta further distinguishes herself by writing about how she intends to become bilingual in the worlds of science and law. When she refers to herself as an "investigator-cum-lawyer" hoping to help resolve the ongoing crisis between pharmaceutical companies and the people of developing countries, the reader is given a specific mental image of what this bilingual scientist-lawyer hopes to do with her law degree. This confidence in her own passion really sets her essay apart.

Overall, Gupta's essay is both informed and passionate. Her essay goes beyond just stating an interest in law school. She immerses the reader into the world of intellectual property law, and she successfully communicates why she is passionate about it.

—*Dennis Ojogho*

PEYTON MILLER

At lunch one day in high school, I was telling a few friends about my summer harvesting tomatoes on a farm. When I began explaining how the vegetables I picked were sold at a nearby gas station, one of my friends corrected me, pointing out that a tomato is a fruit. "Right," I responded, "but it's taxed as a vegetable."

This obscure fact is one among many I absorbed during my boyhood as I listened to my father and grandfather, one a real estate lawyer and the other an entrepreneur, discuss taxation and its impact on business. Thanks to the two of them, and my study of American political history, I have been fascinated by tax policy from an early age. Since high school I have paid close attention to media coverage of tax law, particularly the Bush tax cuts and the perpetual debate over a proposed income tax in my native Tennessee.

When I signed up for a course on American economic policy last spring, I thought I already had a pretty solid understanding of the subject matter, especially when it came to taxation. I could not have been more wrong. What I learned in that class, which is one of the best I have taken in college, was largely theoretical information that required a background in economics. But the biggest surprise to me was the prevalence of federal tax expenditures, exemptions in the tax code that subsidize private sector activities from charitable giving to the production of alternative forms of energy. Taken together, the professor explained, tax expenditures constitute over $1 trillion in foregone revenue each year, requiring much higher overall tax rates. While they can be useful in certain circumstances, tax expenditures often introduce perverse incentives. Many economists are concerned, for example, that the tax exemption for employer-provided medical insurance may contribute to the skyrocketing cost of health care.

I had understood that the tax code included some special preferences, but I had no idea they existed on such an enormous scale. My surprise came partly from the fact that the tax expenditure concept is easy for someone with even a passing knowledge of economics to understand. How could a person like me, who had followed national tax debates for years, have missed such a fundamental aspect of tax policy?

The answer, I think, lies in the fact that the press tends to focus on personalities and moral values, and often provides only rudimentary analysis of policy. In the recent debate over the federal budget deficit, for example, politicians have generally advocated either higher tax rates or cuts in conventional spending, and the media for the most part has acted as if these were the only two alternatives. Few outside academia have raised the possibility of rolling back tax expenditures, which could reduce the deficit without a tax rate increase.

Whether or not this is the best solution, the public should understand that it is an option. As an undergraduate writer and editor, I have tried to educate myself about the nuts and bolts of government to inform Harvard students and the broader public about issues like tax expenditures that often escape media attention. In the summer of 2010, I led a team of writers in developing the *Annual Report of the United States*, a comprehensive explanation of how federal tax dollars are spent. My own writing in publications like *The Harvard Crimson* has explored topics that impact people's day-to-day lives, like the use of variable tolls by municipal governments to mitigate traffic congestion, and ways of reforming organ donation to reduce health-care costs and relieve suffering.

In my professional career, I hope to help improve American government primarily by influencing the policymaking process directly, for which a technical understanding of the law will be crucial. But I also intend to continue what I have started in college: explaining to a broad audience how state action affects citizens. After spending the next several years studying the law and becoming a more effective communicator, I expect to leave law school better able to help others make informed political decisions.

Analysis

The most successful feature of this essay is its clear progression. This is achieved by maintaining a common theme throughout, and not a common one at that: the American tax code. Transitioning from high school memories to college studies to extracurricular involvement and finally, to career prospects, Peyton Miller imbues his essay with a very logical order. Not only does this guide the reader through the piece, but it also makes Miller's professed passion for the tax code much more believable. It is easy to see how high school experiences with entrepreneurship developed into an interest for economics, for example, or how a concern with the media's portrayal of taxation led to an interest in student journalism.

While Miller does not fully delve into an academic discussion of the tax code, he conveys his knowledge of the subject matter very effectively given the space constraints. He does this by weaving in discussion of the different aspects of the tax code with different elements of his life. For example, he uses his experiences growing up in Tennessee to discuss taxes on a local level, then uses his academic studies to approach the subject from an economics perspective, and finally uses his extracurricular involvement to explain the tax code from the perspective of journalism. This allows Miller to develop his personality on the page at the same time as he showcases his knowledge of the American tax code.

One point where the essay could improve is in explaining how law school is related to Miller's interests. Only in the last paragraph is this question addressed: Miller explains "a technical understanding of the law will be crucial" to his career path, and that he hopes to become "a more effective communicator" while in law school. In contrast to the rest of the essay, which is very focused, these two points sound like generalities. In other words, Miller demonstrates he is an interesting individual, but not why he is an interesting individual for law school admissions officers. It might have been more effective to weave law school into this essay earlier on, rather than as a final side note.

On the whole, however, this is a solid essay that future applicants can learn a lot from. The use of a chronological structure combined with an unusual theme is an effective strategy, which lets an applicant's voice shine through. The essay achieves just the right balance between academic discourse and personal recollections.

—*Sarah Fellay*

VICTORIA ABRAHAM

Forced marriage, rape, malnutrition, and drunken teachers offering gifts in exchange for sex; one after the other, girls voiced the barriers they face in trying to complete primary school in Gulu District, Northern Uganda. Their Ugandan audience mirrored the girls' stoic delivery, receiving the information without so much as a gasp. I was part of that audience. As an intern reporter for Mega FM, I had already heard of these barriers from government officials I had previously interviewed throughout my internship. However, it was heartbreaking to hear it spoken by the children who faced these issues daily. Their experiences reminded me of a law course I took in the third year of my combined Journalism and Canadian Studies undergraduate degree at Carleton University, Social Justice and Human Rights.

This course was more challenging than my practical journalism courses, which demanded that excellent research and writing skills, and efficient multitasking were executed within tight deadlines. In this course we studied cosmopolitan and international law, and it was Hannah Arendt's *Eichmann in Jerusalem* and her essay, "The Decline of the Nation-State and the End of the Rights of Man," that were a revelation for me. Arendt argues that the most fundamental human right is the right to have rights, which is only possible when one belongs to an organized political community with the capacity and mandate to protect human rights. She asserts that when people possess this right they are judged by their actions and opinions, rather than by their identity and characteristics. Her exploration of the concepts of statelessness, citizenship, and human rights, and whether those rights are inalienable, crystallized for me the importance of citizenship, the role and responsibilities of states, and the relationship between the two with the rule of law.

As I listened to those Ugandan girls, I heard the devastating consequences brought about by the lack of an organized political community invested with the capacity and mandate to protect human rights. The more people I interviewed and the more I traveled around the Northern region, the more I saw how gendered, systemic barriers to education, employment, and family planning undermined the citizenship and human rights of Ugandan women and children. I witnessed how the lack of an organized political community, and the government's inability to provide basic services such as clean water, contributed to the further eradication of the rights of the most vulnerable. Arendt's assertion of the right to have rights took on a new salience and my passion for women's rights and international law was solidified.

But Arendt's concepts are close to my heart for another reason as well. In 1999, my parents and I immigrated to Canada from Moscow, Russia. For my Nigerian father and myself, Russia was a place where we were more likely to be judged based on our identity and characteristics, rather than on our actions and opinions. In a country where police and justice systems are highly corruptible and a Caucasian skin tone is the best insurance for legal and social equity, the state offered us little protection. Racism was personified in the skinhead who stared at me menacingly during recess at school, and the fear that my mother felt for my father when walking down the street. This changed with our arrival in Canada. Although we had to adjust to a radically different sociopolitical environment, it was a climate without the constant danger, uncertainty, and fear that was such a mainstay throughout our time in Russia. When we received our citizenship, it was further affirmation of belonging and protection.

I chose journalism as my undergraduate degree to enrich my reporting and analytical skills and pursue my passion for writing. I took full advantage of my degree to gain useful skills: I interviewed inspiring people and told the stories of refugees, activists, and entrepreneurs. However, I realized that while journalists hold tremendous power through their ability to bring to light stories that would otherwise remain unknown, they have little power to bring about lasting change. I want to help create lasting change. During my time at Carleton, I tailored my degree to focus on social issues such as immigration policy and women's rights, and I took on a second major, Canadian studies, to gain a greater understanding of Canadian politics and society. My academic and professional choices were driven by my continuous search for a fulfilling academic and professional life. However, it was in Uganda that I realized I still lacked the challenge and purpose I desired.

As a result of my experiences, I have a keen interest in the relationship between international law, citizenship, and human rights. I believe Harvard Law School will provide the education and opportunities to help me build the human and social capital necessary to make a lasting difference in society. Armed with this knowledge, I want to fight for the rights of people, like those Ugandan girls, who cannot fight for themselves. I believe my unique academic and professional skillset and international experiences will contribute to the diversity of Harvard's community in a very productive way.

Analysis

In this essay, Victoria Abraham uses a personal experience unrelated to school in order to establish a persuasive argument defending her interest in law school. Abraham plays to the emotional nature of her narrative in her first sentence when she lists the injustices suffered by Ugandan schoolgirls in the city where she worked. The sentence is dynamic, and it paves the way for the essay to come. Abraham creates a relevant transition into her personal life as an immigrant in order to relate her story about Ugandan students to her own life. By creating this connection, she can make a more convincing argument as to why she was so impacted by the story of the Ugandan students—and better yet, why she wants to make helping these students a professional mission.

Abraham does an excellent job of clarifying why exactly she wants to go to law school. She makes it sound as if law school is absolutely essential to enact the change she wants to see in Africa. She backs this up by talking about her academic interests, and specifying how her coursework at Carleton University was tailored specifically to her experiences in Uganda.

One of the only aspects of this essay that could be strengthened is Abraham's reason for choosing Harvard Law School above other schools. She just points out that Harvard would provide her with opportunities to use her social capital to make a difference in society. It would have been better if she had mentioned a particular feature unique to Harvard Law School that would help her with her goals as opposed to generically stating that the school could help her make a difference. This is only a minor point, however, because the majority of space for this personal statement was used to flesh out Abraham's background and primary interests.

—Charlotte Smith

NICHOLAS WARTHER

Juan Rivera was interrogated for four days before he confessed to the murder of Holly Staker in 1992. On the night of the fourth day, the questioning became particularly accusatory, and he suffered an emotional breakdown. Police found Rivera, a former special-needs student, beating his head against the wall of his jail cell. He was asked again if he killed Staker. Rivera nodded. He signed a typed confession detailing his supposed account of the murder, but when the State's Attorney read the account, the interrogation was ordered to resume because Rivera's words were so erratic. Aside from the confession, there was no physical evidence linking Rivera to the crime. There were no eyewitnesses. Nevertheless, Rivera would be convicted of murder in 1993 and sentenced to life in prison.

I will never forget January 6, 2012, when Juan Rivera was freed. Almost twenty years after his conviction, DNA evidence was produced that proved his innocence. I remember seeing his picture in the *Chicago Tribune*, where, surrounded by a throng of reporters, he looked triumphant. His usually haggard face, accustomed only to the shadows of jail cells for so long, was now lit up by the sun. When I was an intern at the Center on Wrongful Convictions (CWC) the summer after my freshman year, I assisted attorneys who worked tirelessly to free him. Evidence of his guilt seemed so feeble, yet three separate juries were convinced by it. His story still makes me uneasy. With a dearth of evidence against him, how could reasonable people repeatedly consign Rivera to prison for the rest of his life?

I believe there are two sides to every story. So, the next summer I explored the other side of this one by working at the Cook County State's Attorney's Office (SAO). What I learned there astonished me just as much as what I saw at the CWC. Far from being the cold, unfeeling bureaucracy shuffling people through courts and prisons, I saw an organization of people who, for the most part, were doing their jobs carefully and conscientiously. Anita Alvarez, the State's Attorney who is a lightning rod for criticism, struck me as one of these people when she came to speak to our office. She told a story about a woman named Shatoya Currie, or "Girl X," that continues to affect me deeply.

Currie was the victim of a brutal attack in the stairwell of her housing project. "Brutal" is a euphemism—Currie was beaten so badly that she was left completely blind and paralyzed. Miraculously though, after months of agonizing recovery, she progressed to the point where she could communicate by moving her head. This enabled her to identify her attacker, and Alvarez brought the case to trial in 2001. Interestingly, the alleged attacker was defended by lawyers affiliated with the CWC. Alvarez recalled that Currie's testimony was particularly heart wrenching, as she had to spell out every one of her words with facial movements. Her tormented account had a profound impact on the jurors, and Alvarez's face lit up with satisfaction when she told this part. When Currie was told about the guilty verdict, she smiled the "biggest smile you could imagine." I could see why. If the man was truly guilty, then Currie finally had justice and the security of knowing that her attacker was behind bars.

These two experiences—at the CWC and the SAO—revealed to me the many shades of gray that color our legal system. When the difference between life in prison and freedom hinges on the testimony of a few witnesses, a rigorous examination of evidence is necessary. In college, I have been drawn to the field of statistics, which gets to the very heart of the legal issues raised by the cases described above. Statistics quantifies the uncertainties in those verdicts as a type I or type II error. A type I error occurs when a true hypothesis is incorrectly rejected—sending an innocent man to jail—as in Rivera's case. A type II error occurs when a false hypothesis is wrongly accepted—letting a guilty man go free, which could have happened in the Currie case. Legal judgments boil down to deciding which error is worse. Setting the threshold for how certain we need to be of a person's guilt to convict them higher increases the probability of a type II error (e.g., letting a murderer walk the streets), and setting the threshold lower increases the probability of a type I error (e.g., convicting an innocent person).

How could an innocent man like Rivera be convicted three times and sentenced to jail? After hearing the Shatoya Currie story, I realized it was because the juries decided that the risk of a type II error was too great—perhaps they saw a girl like Currie in his case, too, and they decided that the possibility of letting her attacker go free posed a greater threat than the possibility of sending an innocent Rivera to jail. The need to answer these complex and unsettling questions is why I have known since the beginning of high school that I would be a lawyer. Looking at life's vagaries head-on and making them accountable to reason fascinates me, and I believe that statistics provides me with a unique background to do so.

Analysis

Nicholas Warther begins his personal statement with a moving account of a man coerced into a false confession, wrongfully convicted of murder, and imprisoned for nearly twenty years before DNA evidence led to his exoneration. He goes on to describe the experience of a woman beaten so brutally that she was left blind and paralyzed; her cause was aided by the Cook County State's Attorney's Office, an organization Warther was surprised to find full of thoughtful, conscientious staff. Warther's interest in pursuing a career in the law is unmistakable: The courtroom is the stage on which we punish the guilty (and, hopefully, protect the innocent), and it's the one that he wants to work on.

In addition to demonstrating a passion for justice, Warther conveys a nuanced understanding of the problems that characterize legal decision making. He brings his knowledge of statistics to bear on the moral and practical dilemma facing judges and lawyers: How much evidence do we need before we can be certain of a defendant's guilt beyond a reasonable doubt? What's worse—locking up too many people (through type I errors) or letting too many people walk free (through type II errors)? Implicit is the pressing issue of the trade-off society faces between individual liberty and collective security.

Warther's essay is logically constructed, well written, and interesting to read. But while he does an excellent job of showcasing his interest in becoming a lawyer, the picture he paints of himself lacks depth. It was wise for him to emphasize his fondness for statistics—this quantitative dimension sets him apart from most of the legal applicant pool. Still, had he condensed his discussion of Rivera's and Currie's cases, he would have had space to give the admissions officer a better sense of his personal background and interests beyond the legal realm.

Although lacking a full discussion in that respect, the essay does manage to present a thinking and multidimensional Nicholas Warther. The juxtaposition of internships risks feeling contrived, but Warther's discussion shows he has thought thoroughly about these contrasts and these issues. His essay displays a passion for the law and for analyzing its ambiguities and facets. Naturally, that makes for a good law school candidate.

—*Lisa Mogilanski*

THE WORLD

If you want to attend law school and become a lawyer, you need a desire to learn. For many applicants, the greatest opportunity to learn has been time spent in diverse parts of the world, and the content of that learning has shaped who they are. These essays jet from Madagascar to El Salvador to Korea and back to the United States, showing how their writers have grown by engaging the multifaceted world around them.

But these essays also run a very real risk of coming across as trite and cliché. Simply having an experience (or even many experiences) outside your home country doesn't stand out on its own, and the list of essays involving service activities abroad is a long and at times monotonous one. Statistically speaking, you've probably lived the majority of your life within U.S. borders, and it's more than fine to draw from domestic life. No need to include an experience abroad for the sake of including an experience abroad. Trust us, admissions officers have seen it before.

As a general rule you should consider shying away from this sort of topic, especially if your experiences say more about the place you've visited than they do about you. Not even the successful essays in this section are immune from this essay type's pitfalls. However, if you have had a fresh experience worth sharing, and if you frame it right, showing how you've learned from the heterogeneity around you can make for a worthwhile essay.

MARISA SCHNAITH

I arrived at Zulaa's home as her moans of pain filled the one-room house, blood soaked the bed, and the dogs and goats outside started barking and bleating. I had spent my life with my nose in a book, but now here I was with my nose between her legs, watching a new life enter this tiny Mongolian village. Hours later, I had helped clean beautiful baby Sarnai and dispose of the bloody towels in the outhouse. When the midwife took her leave, I took a moment to reflect. How had my central-Ohio suburban upbringing, full of study and rigorous academic pursuits, led me to my—now—good friend Zulaa's bedside, squeezing her hand and offering encouraging Mongolian words with every contraction?

I grew up in the middle-class suburbs of Powell, Ohio, a place I both lovingly and regretfully came to know as the "Powell Bubble." When I began my undergraduate studies among the conservative student body at Miami University, I was determined to step outside "the Bubble." Initially, I explored my interest in diverse groups of people and lifestyles through coursework such as Arab Nationalism in World Politics, and Development of the Soviet Policy. Encouraged by these courses to expand my learning beyond the classroom walls, I studied abroad in Argentina and Spain.

I brought my study abroad home through volunteer work at Su Casa in Cincinnati and creation of an after-school Spanish program for a local second-grade class. This connection to the Latino culture inspired my selection of the 2007 abortion reform in Mexico City as the subject for my senior honors thesis. I studied the reproductive laws of Mexico City and the history of politics and social activism that allowed for this reform to occur. Seeing a few strong voices effect such change, this research encouraged my interest in the law, specifically as it relates to human rights.

Excited by this new focus, I wrote a grant to the honors program and received funds to join the Students for Peace and Social Justice Delegation to Guatemala. Through our meetings with indigenous groups, women's rights organizers, and local authorities struggling with immigration issues, we witnessed firsthand the inequalities and human rights abuses occurring there. At Miami I shared my experience in various classes and campus events, and also presented on Guatemalan violence for the final project in my honors Warfare and Violence in the Bible course.

After college graduation, I sought an experience that would further cultivate my growing passion for human rights, public service, and international perspective. When I received an invitation to teach English in Mongolia for the Peace Corps, I was thrilled to have an opportunity to experience a new part of the world. The challenges of living in rural Mongolia were great, but I learned to thrive inside my Ger, building fires in my wood-burning stove as one of the deadliest Mongolian winters in over a decade raged outside. When my site mate decided to return to America after one year of service, she left me the only foreigner and native English speaker in over a hundred miles. I persevered, however, and opted to extend my service by two months to work with a fellow volunteer in implementing a six-week intensive English training for employees of Mongolia's National Emergency Management Agency.

And so I found myself in the final spring of my service, holding baby Sarnai, reflecting on my accomplishments. I made the sort of friends that ask you to attend the birth of their first daughter. I built bridges between the seemingly incompatible Powell Bubble and rural Mongolia. I equipped people with the confidence and tools they needed to pursue their dreams. Zulaa was an out-of-work mother of three, living in a town most cannot pronounce and in a country unknown to many. However, with the English I taught her and, more importantly, the confidence I helped her find in herself, she and her husband pursued one of their dreams to coordinate with the international charity, Samaritan's Purse, to bring gifts and basic necessities to the children of over fifty local Mongolian families.

My relationship with Zulaa taught me that one person's passion and commitment can make a difference in others' lives. With its commitment to the importance of public service and international connectedness, Harvard Law is the perfect environment for me. Harvard's extensive partnerships in the semester abroad program, the Summer Public Interest Funding program, and the Human Rights program all present an exciting chance to combine my passion for public service work with my interest in international cultures. The breadth of courses, clinics, and externships offered at

Harvard provide the opportunity I am looking for to explore my interests and share my experiences and perspectives. Further, the Bernard Koteen Office of Public Interest Advising will equip me with the tools I need to pursue a career in public service. Growing up deep in the countryside of Mongolia, baby Sarnai Marisa Nam-srai will serve as a reminder of how I once touched someone's life and made a difference.

Analysis

Press pause for a moment, and before figuring out why Marisa Schnaith's essay is successful, let us figure out what we know about her after reading her essay. What does each paragraph say, and what does that mean about Marisa Schnaith?

Schnaith worked in an environment very different from her hometown in Ohio—rural Mongolia; we know that she's had very diverse experiences. She describes her will to expand her horizons beyond the homogeneous community she grew up in; so Schnaith's diverse experiences are a product of her own curiosity and initiative. She talks about volunteer work and academic interest in Latin America; we learn that she is passionate about human rights and this passion has spurred her interest in law. The fifth paragraph is about her experience in Mongolia with the Peace Corps and the sixth paragraph is about the value she found in her experience. From these two paragraphs we know Schnaith is capable of hard work in a harsh environment, and that she turned her passion for human rights into a tangible accomplishment. In the final paragraph Schnaith talks about making a difference in people's lives, and her interest in specific programs at Harvard. Schnaith wants to make a difference, and Schnaith has spent time and energy figuring out what specific opportunities Harvard has to offer.

In short, Schnaith is curious and hardworking, she takes initiative, she's had challenging experiences in other countries, and she's passionate about human rights. Sounds like someone I'd want to be my lawyer! We know a lot about Schnaith, but how? Did she ever explicitly say, "I am curious and hardworking!"? Of course she didn't say that; if she had we probably wouldn't believe her without evidence to back it up. The reason Schnaith's essay is successful is that she communicates a lot about herself without plainly stating her qualities. Schnaith couldn't just claim that she's passionate about human rights and that she wants to be a lawyer, she had to take us through her experiences so that we understand and believe her. Apart from being well written and interesting, the success of Schnaith's essay can be boiled down to two things: First, she communicates a lot about herself, and second, she does so by showing the reader what it is about her life and her actions that make her who she is and make her want to apply to law school.

—*Eliza Hale*

WILLIAM BARLOW II

An old, dough-faced woman with white-blond hair and soft, sagging limbs spots us from a distance and darts inside her home. Behind the window she waits. Her wrinkled, veiny hands crack an opening in the blinds as she peers down at us. Two strange young men in suits and white shirts knock on her neighbor's door. I have seen what she has done, but pretend not to notice. Usually, it will make it less awkward.

Still, everyone deserves a chance, and I have been wrong more than once in my suspicions that someone is deliberately avoiding us. No one answers at the present door, so we walk over to hers. It is a light-yellow home with a cheery, red birdhouse and a mat with the word VÄLKOMMEN! imprinted in curly, black letters. I knock on the door. The woman reappears, and before I have a chance to say a word she lets loose a torrent of Swedish.

"Hello. I know why you're here, and I'm not interested," she proclaims with her face turned away, her hand clinging firmly to the doorknob. I amiably say that we understand, and the two of us turn to leave. As we walk to the next house I gently wave to her as she once again peers through the pane. She probably does not know who we are. People mostly guess that we are the Jehovah's Witnesses, who canvass the town regularly. Mormon missionaries have not been to this area in well over five years.

It is a rare treat to spend an afternoon meandering through neighborhoods of detached houses. Most days find us marching through large apartment complexes. The encounters there tend to be less uniform and prosaic than their counterparts in the suburbs. The first door may produce a veiled woman from Somalia, the second a mild-mannered Chinese student, the third a pink and somewhat drunken Croatian man with a good deal to say on the subject of religion, which he feels the need to repeat several times to drive his point home. There is something altogether refreshing about meeting such a broad spectrum of people, serving them, and taking with us some small part of their ethnic and religious viewpoints.

These and other missionary experiences have been invaluable to my personal development. Foremost, I have a greater appreciation for people whose perspectives are different from my own. I learned the importance of relentless, dedicated hard work—waking up daily at 6:30 A.M. to study and learn Swedish and pursue other vital studies. The many hours spent each day knocking on doors and talking to people on the street taught me perseverance and an understanding of how to deal with those who may be unfriendly or even combative. Being required to work in tandem with a missionary companion 24/7, I learned tolerance and the value of teamwork. As a district leader, I was given responsibility over a group of missionaries spread out over three cities and 150 miles apart, with the charge to lead, encourage, and advise them, enhancing my administrative, motivational, counseling, and interpersonal skills.

Upon returning to Duke, I was better prepared to take advantage of the opportunities available to me there. Wanting to utilize my language skills, I enrolled in a semester abroad to conduct extensive research for my senior honors thesis, accessing primary sources only available in Swedish. Delving into arguments between Social Democratic leaders, I began tracking the party's early ideological shifts and relating them to its later success. I became more engaged with groups on campus as well, becoming first a voracious writer for the Duke College Republicans and eventually the director of its blog. I also reawakened my passion for creative writing and began submitting stories to online journals.

My life experiences have helped me develop the attributes of an industrious work ethic, a determination to make a difference, and a commitment to help others. From speaking with lawyers and law students, watching appellate court arguments, and reading full court opinions, I find the law fascinating. I very much look forward to dedicating my full efforts to law school.

Analysis

This essay makes fantastic use of a personal narrative about one specific experience. The first part of William Barlow's essay is completely dedicated to retelling a story about his mission trip in Sweden. It is not immediately clear where the story takes place, or what Barlow is doing, but the gradual revealing of information is engaging enough to make the reader question why this is relevant to Barlow's story. The reader can get a sense of Barlow's personality through stories about his tenacity while on his mission, his writing style, and the activities he busied himself with upon his return.

Barlow also does a good job with tying his personal experiences together with his coursework. He says that his experiences abroad dealing with difficult people on his mission trip and researching Swedish politics encouraged him to write both creatively and noncreatively for several on-campus political groups. The emphasis in this essay isn't necessarily coursework-related. It is centered on Barlow's work ethic, which he thinks makes him an ideal candidate for law school. He uses specific experiences and encounters to reveal that work ethic, as well as his openness of thought and appreciation of diversity.

Barlow does leave a gap in omitting his religion, opting only for the indirect reference to himself as a Mormon missionary. But the fact that he chose to discuss his experience as a missionary suggests that his religion—the driving purpose behind that experience—must play an equally important role in explaining who he is. A personal statement certainly doesn't need to touch on religion. Yet Barlow's statement refuses the briefest discussion even as it invites it.

Even so, Barlow does use a rare, rich set of experiences to illustrate his qualifications and his potential. The reader might finish the essay wanting to know more about Barlow, but the most important points—who he is, who he can become—are clear and convincing.

—*Charlotte Smith*

LARA BERLIN

The dust swirls around our Land Rover as we roll down the bumpy streets of Kailahun, the town on the eastern border of Sierra Leone where the brutal civil war erupted over sixteen years earlier. Broken down on the side of the road is an old military tanker, a remnant serving as a constant reminder of a conflict fueled by viciousness, helplessness, and fear. Yet today this particular image is not solely one of tragedy, for it has been transformed into a productive element of daily life in the most unexpected of ways—as a clothesline with pants, shirts, and even bras draped over the collapsed military machinery to dry. I laugh at what had become a familiar experience—the nuanced irony of life frequently overlooked by mainstream media.

In fact, it is that nuanced reality—one in which apparent dichotomies may be false shadows hiding a dynamic and fluid world—which I have always called home. I grew up in a very egocentric culture in Southern California while practicing a sociocentric Native American spirituality. My rigorous academic engagement never made me forget the importance of forging powerful emotional connections. As a young white woman I often felt most at home in predominantly black communities. Inspired by my early experiences breaking false barriers, I felt an immutable calling beginning at a very young age to reach out to people around the world who had been oppressed by the imposition of such obstacles. Nothing seemed more important.

I began my quest with a purely humanitarian approach through local community service projects and cultural exchanges to Latin America. Over the ensuing years, the more I witnessed as I worked in the slums of Kenya, the post-conflict towns of Sierra Leone, and the ghettos of San Francisco, the more I came to realize that it was not merely through poverty reduction efforts such as building houses that these walls of oppression could be demolished. I attempted to incorporate into my approach the listening skills taught to me by my psychologist parents, the strength and compassion shown to me in my studies of nonviolence movements, and the grassroots mobilization demonstrated by various organizations with whom I had worked. The people I met in the communities in which I served awed me with their consistent displays of generosity and receptivity, despite the adversity they faced. However, I was stymied by the complex and deep-rooted sociopolitical dynamics that rendered the window into resolving those adversities opaque. I found myself repeatedly faced with the question, "What can we do?" While the passion to serve was ever present, discovering the way to systemically transform the military tanker into a clothesline was proving elusive.

Only in exploring this question in environments in which the laws were not clearly defined or obeyed did I realize the importance of the law in providing the necessary transformative paradigm. Law is the backbone of society—that which engraves the protection of human dignity into the rules governing our daily lives. When social change remains at the purely grassroots level (as has been the folly of many attempted movements), that change is subject to the whim of those governing that particular locality. Thus, the change, and the manifestation of the human rights it embodies, can be fleeting. Fundamental to lasting provisions for human dignity and a peaceful global coexistence is the formulation and enforcement of laws that reflect these values.

I recognize the complexity involved in all legal processes, particularly in the realm of conflict resolution in which all too often one must weigh peace against justice in order to achieve one's ends. Yet it is through the very complexity of debating legal agreements such as these that one can transcend formerly insurmountable and oppressive barriers. Hence, I have come to passionately embrace law as the primary vehicle through which I can promote profound global change. I anticipate the opportunity to study law with the same immutable calling I felt as a child, except this time that calling is grounded in a deeper understanding of the challenges to be faced complemented by my unwavering hope for humanity.

Analysis

Beginning in *medias res*, Lara Berlin's essay takes the reader across three continents in chronicling the author's steadfast determination to end the "apparent dichotomies . . . hiding a dynamic and fluid world." The article begins with the image of clothing hanging from a rusting tank and the "nuanced irony" of the intersection of destruction and urban renewal is the primary theme in Berlin's essay.

Berlin begins by describing the qualifications that she possesses that best prepare her to posit on such a difficult topic. She begins with her experience breaking down racial barriers as a child in Southern California—feeling more at home in communities of different races and adopting an unusual Native American spiritual focus.

One of Berlin's main strengths throughout is her ability to focus the essay around one theme and appropriately tie back each essay to the overarching idea. In this case, it is "an immutable calling . . . to reach out to people around the world who had been oppressed" by the institution of socioeconomic and racial barriers. Berlin flawlessly segues from her childhood to her adult life—working from Latin America to Africa in a series of poverty reduction efforts intended to effect change from the ground level.

However, Berlin finds an unresolvable conflict: She cannot resolve the generous goals of the organizations she works for with the inefficacy of her work. Feeling a compelling need to help out the people she helped, Berlin turns to the law. Here, she does a good job pivoting back to how this essay relates to HLS. Calling law "the backbone of society," Berlin nicely illustrates both a theory of social change and a compelling reason for the altruistic pursuits she will use her law degree for.

However, while the ideas of the essay flow well, the mechanics are relatively lacking. Berlin often uses inappropriate word choice to characterize her experiences. Confusing verbiage—like the Southern California "egocentric culture" never fully explained or peculiar phrasing of "immutable calling"—prevents the writer from conveying her ideas most effectively.

In sum, Berlin demonstrates a very effective and practical theory of change throughout the essay, using a solid organizational structure and clear ideas to illustrate the process by which she came to pursue law and how she will use her law degree. More than anything, Berlin displays a knowledge of where she came from and where she is going.

—David Freed

DEANNA PARRISH

Nadia invited me to her apartment for what she described as a small "book club" meeting. Instead I found myself in a room overflowing with rural Moroccan women, dusty from hours of travel, eager to discuss the Qu'ran, women's rights, and their relationship to democracy. I was the only woman that did not wear a *hijab*. The only woman who did not speak *Darija*. The only woman who did not see the Arab Spring through the eyes of an Islamic feminist.

I traveled to Morocco to study migration, an intellectual passion inspired by my family's diaspora, having fled Cuba in the early 1960s. This personal history has drawn me to the relationship between changemakers—immigrants, women, and social entrepreneurs—and their environments. While my professors spoke of Morocco's geopolitical nature, I remained fascinated by the issues faced by young women who protested in ever-greater numbers outside of the Parliament building. As a result of my work with various feminist advocacy organizations, direct service providers, and gender-based violence shelters, I met Nadia. Nadia is a legal scholar who led the Islamic feminist effort to reinterpret the text of the Qu'ran. From our conversations I gleaned the first of many reasons motivating me to pursue a legal education: The law is a critical tool.

Morocco is infamous for the *Mudawanna* code, legislation that governs all aspects of family law. Reforms in 2004 established joint responsibility between husbands and wives for their families and introduced family courts to enable the enforcement of these new laws. Amid the energy of the Arab Spring and widespread calls to rewrite the Moroccan constitution, feminist activists found the environment ripe to question the ability of the family courts system to reverse centuries old patterns of gender discrimination. For feminists, little progress had been made outside of the letter of the law. Issues of sex discrimination, polygamy, and intimate partner violence were seldom reported, but remained highly visible at the grassroots level.

Seeking a deeper understanding for the basis of this deep-seated socio-legal conflict, I focused my senior honors thesis on the relationship between the reformed *Mudawanna* code, adjudication in the legal system, and the ultimate effect on women in Moroccan society. This conflict between the law's ability to regulate society ultimately inspired my interest in the law. Legal principles iterate the stories of the disenfranchised, empower communities to advocate for social change, and codify a living body of work that reflects history while ethically informing our future. With knowledge of the law, I will be a champion of political progress and change makers themselves.

My research in Morocco and internship experiences in the public and government sectors have shown me firsthand the limitations of advocating for meaningful change without a complete understanding of its legal foundations. In my future legal career, I will confront complex questions concerning the limitations of the law in affecting social behavior, and the legal response to those limitations. Whether I ultimately apply my legal knowledge to protecting international human rights or advocating on behalf of undocumented immigrants in the United States, I hope to shape how the letter of the law comes to life on the grassroots level.

Analysis

Deanna Parrish's essay not only opens in the midst of her story, but it also quickly and deftly introduces several key themes. The initial lines describe the women and their ideas, which go on to wind throughout the essay. They also pack in a sophisticated motif, the distinct distance between Parrish and her "book club" companions. That marks a level of nuance many travel-based essays don't grasp.

That opening paragraph contains something of Parrish at her best, but it also begets disappointment as the reader moves on. For the most part, we lose Nadia and her book club; we lose the theme of separation between the traveler and the indigenous. The tangible experience of Parrish in Morocco fades into broader, more didactic statements about Moroccan social and legal history. For instance, the entire third paragraph reads more like an encyclopedia entry. The reader learns that Parrish has spent time thinking about these issues, but we don't learn enough about Parrish herself through them. We also don't see a higher level of analysis. Most of

Parrish's commentary and ultimate lesson reduces to a single, basic truism: "The law is a critical tool." It's not a problem to introduce broader ideas and issues that you care about. But it does become a problem if you don't show yourself careful weighing them.

With that said, Parrish does leave the reader with a message and a sense worth imparting: that she is committed. Throughout the essay, in fact, Parrish conveys her motivation and energy. For some essays, a trip abroad becomes simply a nice experience, unconnected to a person's broader trajectory and interests. But in Parrish's case, the experience—and its intersection with the law—constitutes her senior thesis, and she clearly explains how Morocco motivates her. We get the sense that Parrish has spent a lot of time learning and understanding Morocco's women and their issues—all the more a shame that she focuses mainly on recounting and less on analyzing. Further, she understands precisely the significance of a law school education because she understands how the law relates to the issues she cares about. She doesn't want admission for admissions sake; she wants to learn to be a lawyer.

—Brian Cronin

DANIEL MCMANN

I was sweating profusely. Was it the sweltering heat, the spicy *kim-chi*, or the nerves? I'm convinced it was a combination of all three. With bare feet, I sat on the floor with my legs tightly crossed under the stout table. I maneuvered my chopsticks carefully; the last thing I wanted was for my new coteachers, especially the principal, to think poorly of my table manners. I read extensively on Korea's Confucian-rooted dining etiquette before I left for my new life in Seoul. Now I was expected to put this etiquette into practice. It didn't help that my new coteachers hardly spoke a word of English. Equally, the only Korean I could remember was *annyeong haseyo* and *kamsa hamnida*. Accordingly, I found myself greeting and thanking people all too frequently. Life had been simple and comfortable in Canada, but now I was a blond-haired, functionally illiterate foreigner in a strange land who stood out like a sore thumb. A week prior, I had been incredibly thrilled for this opportunity to live abroad, now I was not convinced that moving to Korea was the right decision.

It is always the case that nerves, challenges, and fear of the unknown swing my mood from excitement to pessimism when I begin my travels abroad. Fortunately, this pessimism vanishes rapidly when I am fully immersed in another culture. It is thrilling, mind-opening experiences and meeting new, remarkable people that fuels my passion for traveling. As I walk through the streets of Seoul I find myself learning, like a child, to read again. I can read Hangul, the Korean alphabet, to the point where I can pronounce most words. But, my Korean vocabulary is still severely limited as most Korean words remain meaningless sounds to my ears. As time progresses, I am confident that I will grasp a solid understanding of the language that once seemed to be from a far, inaccessible place. In just weeks, I have had experiences that would be unimaginable in my home country. I have held monkeys in Bangkok, ate pig's nose in Seoul, rode elephants in southern Thailand, and been warned that "Drug trafficking is punishable by death in the Republic of China." I no longer have any doubts that starting a new life teaching English in Korea was the best decision I could have made.

My mother has always told me that "The experiences you have while traveling will be the ones you will always remember." True to her word, the lectures from the first week of university remain fuzzy in my mind, but I can remember nearly every word of conversations I had with Cubans in Havana from my several trips to the tropical island. I even remember the locals ensuring that the door was closed and voices kept down when the conversations turned to sensitive topics, such as politics. I cannot recall many of the Christmas gifts I exchanged with my family, nor the fairs I attended as a child, but I could never forget the Carnaval de Mazatlán in Mexico. Nor could I forget the lights of Las Vegas, the sounds of Times Square, or the thrill of the Space Mountain roller coaster in Disneyland. Equally, I cannot recall the origin or destination of a single taxi ride I have taken in Canada, but I do remember the difficulty I had finding a *tuk-tuk* that would take me directly to my hostel in Bangkok. The fare for taxis in Thailand is very minimal; accordingly, many taxi drivers insist that you make two or three stops en route to your final destination where you are expected to go inside selected stores so the driver can earn a commission. If you wish to see Bangkok for cheap, hire a taxi for pennies to drive you all over the city to different shops; the taxi driver will be more than happy to collect the commissions at every stop and will require only pennies as payment from the passenger.

My experiences relate to a quote from the Harvard Law School's International Legal Studies information page: "At Harvard Law School, 'international' is not just something we teach. It is something we are." I seek to study international law at Harvard Law School through the International and Comparative Law program of study. My travel experience, coupled with my economics degree, set a solid foundation for studying international law, with possible focuses in international trade, law and third world economic development, anti-poverty law, international finance, and business and corporate law. I believe that I would fit well into the Harvard community and will be a valuable member of the International and Comparative Law program.

Analysis

Daniel McMann's enthusiasm for traveling and his love for new mind-opening experiences are evident in his writing. The admissions officer reading this essay can readily see McMann's passion through the way in which he conveys his adventures to the audience. McMann describes a variety of firsthand experiences with vivid detail, although he is sure to drive home the point that he loves traveling and immersing himself in other cultures through a direct statement. Notably, McMann shares the lessons that he has learned from his travels and shows how they have shaped his personality and outlook on life.

A drawback to McMann's essay is that at times it can feel as though he is merely listing all of the places he had traveled. International travel can be a powerful, formative experience—especially for one interested in international law, but an essay should explain how that international exposure informs and influences him. McMann takes the reader on a Cook's tour; we see him encountering a colorful variety of local bits and oddities. We hear him explain how other parts of the world are more exciting than home in Canada. But we don't understand how his ventures are more than travel for the sake of travel. Far too many Harvard Law applicants have international experience to make that a distinguishing factor in itself. How that experience engenders growth is what counts.

What McMann does manage to show is a passion for the world and for exploring it. He clearly hasn't opted for time abroad, whether as a traveler or an English teacher, as filler for a résumé. McMann's most fleshed-out example, his time in Korea, might leave the reader wanting to learn more, but it does showcase his commitment. He struggles with becoming "fully immersed in another culture," and yet he is determined to achieve it.

—*Katherine M. Kulik*

ELIZABETH SPENCER

When I was five, I had a charming habit of running full force into Lake Washington with all my clothes on, whenever I got the chance. This and my tendency to climb any tree whose first branches I could reach tended to make my mother, schoolteachers, and friends' parents a little batty.

I have always been independent, confident, and maybe a little brash.

By the time I could use a phone, I had found more ways of exploring the world. I started a professional theater career at age ten. I wrote a résumé (I was encouraged by my mother not to illustrate the margins with hearts and happy faces), got myself an agent, and started calling audition hotlines. By high school I had performed in eight professional and fringe plays in Seattle, a small handful of movies and public service videos, and one cassette tape called "Fantastikids" where we sang about the dangers of mean kids and wine coolers. I was rejected over and over. I learned to eat ramen noodles fast between homework and showtime. I named my mother's puppy Shakespeare. I learned not to feel dejected if I didn't get a part.

By the time I could drive, I had to fly to get where I was going. I went to Nicaragua and Costa Rica the third trimester of my senior year in high school. In lieu of calculus, I vaccinated baby cows from anthrax. In Nicaragua I lived in a house with a dirt floor, no water or electricity, and no bathroom (we used the neighbor's outhouse, climbing under barbed wire to get there), and worked with the family to build a community well. In Costa Rica I helped Dan Jansen, an ecologist from the University of Pennsylvania, research caterpillars—wading rivers in rubber boots and plucking the poor creatures from their leafy homes. I learned I could go anywhere.

My inclination to fling myself into the world has sometimes bordered on foolhardy. As I boarded the plane to Taiwan on a fellowship the summer between my junior and senior year at Brown, I had only a name of a professor who would pick me up from the airport and the vague idea that I was going to Taiwan to study forests and storms. It did not strike me as problematic that I spoke no Chinese, nor knew where I would stay the first night there. It was. For three months I would be unable to eat, travel, or do my research without help. Yet somehow everything was fine. I was lucky to have a cadre of Taiwanese grad students who took me under their collective broken-English wing. Hung-min taught me what a night market was, how to climb Syue Mountain, and gave me the essential words I needed: "dumpling," "milk tea," and "I don't speak Chinese." I helped Hung-min brave Typhoon Haitang for three days to collect stream samples for his research, while wearing hard hats. One night I taught him how to swim. Taiwan taught me dependence and gratitude.

Now, finally, I am learning patience. Working with Native American tribes for EPA means holding meetings where all forty people face in a circle, and everyone is granted the opportunity to speak. It means slow progress mired by past broken promises from the federal government. It means spending the first part of any conversation talking about parents and grandchildren, fry bread, and where we came from. Make the meeting quick; dive into the problem; accomplish the task—these I can do. Listen; gain trust; accomplish the first step—these I've had to learn.

To Harvard, I bring the urge to dive in with all my clothes on, the patience to learn, and gratitude for the opportunity. I bring the urge to keep learning all I can, so that I can one day meld an understanding of the natural environment with legal skills, and emerge to practice environmental law. Finally, to Harvard I bring a mean recipe for fry bread, a foolproof way to test the pH of storm water, and a tendency to climb any tree whose first branches I can reach.

Analysis

Elizabeth Spencer's writing is both personal, making readers feel as if we have gotten to know her, and engaging, making us want to know her better. She shows, rather than tells, that she is passionate, creative, and ready to take the initiative. While she does discuss her research and several of her achievements, it doesn't come off as boastful, and doesn't regurgitate her résumé. Spencer makes it clear that she genuinely cares about her work through the choice anecdotes she includes. Her essay also effectively uses humor, giving it personality and making it enjoyable for the reader.

Spencer puts a comic twist on all her achievements, but this does not detract from their significance. She seems somewhat dismissive of the obstacles she has faced by humorously describing her inability to speak Chinese and living in a dirt-floored hut. However, this approach is much more successful than if she had tried to make her experience seem too dramatic or life-changing. By downplaying her struggles, Spencer actually shows that she overcame significant obstacles by being able to talk about them lightly; she is able to laugh about her experiences. Furthermore, this style makes her seem like not only a successful researcher and student, but more importantly, an interesting person.

This piece covers a long period of time, from her childhood through her time in college. While most essays center on a specific event or story, Spencer opts for a wider scope, which does run into the pitfall of becoming redundant. A stronger essay might offer less variety of experience and go into those experiences in more depth in order to get at more aspects of who she has become.

Of course, the essay doesn't make the mistake of trying to be an autobiography of everything that happened in Spencer's life but rather the different stories work together to paint a picture of her as someone who is adventurous and willing to take risks and try something new. Spencer lays out her anecdotes in a clear progression; they demonstrate her growth in maturity and understanding. She learns to take the initiative, to not be disheartened by failure, to depend on and work with others, and the importance of patience in achieving her goals. While this essay is tied together by her impulsive behavior, Spencer makes it clear that she has the necessary maturity and experience of a successful law student.

—Caroline Zhang

JOSHUAH FIVESON

Law influences virtually every aspect of the world and works, in theory, to ensure equality and justice for those which it governs, serving as a safety net for societal values. Yet within this fail-safe, the very moral fabric that society relies upon, exist areas in which people become entangled and rendered unable to function. This delicately woven safeguard becomes yet another barrier, preventing those who lack the means to successfully navigate it, helpless. Attorneys are the integral artisans who, through their expertise of the law, transcend these barriers and ultimately serve as the gatekeepers between justice in theory and in reality. As national borders slowly dissolve along the global, political, and economic fronts, the need for legal professionals from diverse backgrounds becomes more and more of a necessity.

My life has taken me around the globe—from ancient monasteries now deep under the waters of the Three Gorges Valley in China, to remnants of Incan cities in Peru—allowing me to see people, places, and things others may never get the chance to experience, while shaping my perceptions of the world we live in. Recently, I found myself within the depths of the Panamanian rain forest, a land fraught with danger and beauty, opportunity and deprivation, and memories that will resonate within me forever. En route to the various villages and schools in desperate need of food, the hills slowly became alive as men, women, and children gathered. Just as I had witnessed time and time again throughout my travels—there was an unspoken divide, a mental obstruction, separating "us" from "them." Disregarding these superficial differences I reached out to the people, greeting them in their native dialect and shattering any preconceptions they had already formed. Surprised that I wasn't just another foreigner, they opened up. Children began scurrying down the hills on small footpaths; eagerly grabbing at the packages of food we had hauled through the jungle. Their eyes lighting up in excitement, as it was an uncommon thing to see outsiders in those regions of the country. It was only at the end of my journey that I realized I was able to do what many in this world cannot. I was able to transcend the barriers that plague the minds, hearts, and lives of millions. The barricade that lays between those that have and those that do not; those that can and those that cannot; those who aspire and those that lay impotent in defeat. These impediments contribute to the many problems that our society faces, creating obstructions that can ultimately impact the course of a person's life, for better or for worse.

Although my first semester at Tulane University Law School has been exceptionally stimulating, I am drawn to Harvard Law School for a host of reasons—the fundamental basis of which being the strength of its internationally focused programs. I find myself invigorated by the prospect of participating in your International Human Rights Clinic and working with such renowned scholars such as professors Giannini and Roseman. I am also particularly interested in taking courses with Professor Delgato, given his breadth of scholarship on human rights issues in South America. Furthermore, the variety of internationally oriented research programs offered at Harvard speaks directly to my envisaged career path. Although Tulane Law School is widely known for its international cachet in certain arenas, its academic offerings relating to my intended field of practice are clearly lacking in light of the seemingly tailored programs that Harvard has to offer. To this extent, I feel that I lack the necessary resources that will allow me to develop my full potential within the field. Likewise, Harvard's location provides access to unique opportunities that are not currently available to me in New Orleans. Although the city of New Orleans has a depth of cultural and historical offerings, Cambridge provides practical access to multiple internationally influential cities such as Boston, New York, and Washington, D.C., and to be frank—I did not come to law school to sightsee. My travels well off the beaten path have resulted in an expanded understanding of the interpersonal interactions and relationships that contour the modern global arena. As such, I want to leverage this unique, real world experience into the public sector.

Upon matriculation to Harvard I will have traveled to over ten countries and began studying a third language, allowing me to bring a unique world perspective to my studies and even further, my future work as an attorney. I will bring a singular level of passion, dedication, and real-world experience distinguishable from my contemporaries, and I feel this confluence of skills and attributes will allow me to significantly strengthen, and diversify, the class of 2014. Though I cannot claim myself to be an altruist guided only by selfless intentions, I do on the other hand know where my fidelity lies and where my skills, life experiences, and personal drive would be best utilized. I ask not simply to attend Harvard Law School for the implied recompense such entitlement confers. I want to be an influencing agent, to impact our system—the rational balance of our world—for the better. One case at a time.

Analysis

Because Joshuah Fiveson isn't a standard first-year applicant, his essay naturally takes on a different purpose than most other applicants essays would. For this reason, he devotes much of his essay to explaining his reasons for transfer, focusing in particular on the established prestige and opportunities offered by Harvard's international programs. To this end, he vividly describes his time abroad and details the experiences and people he encountered on these trips. Most importantly, he effectively articulates the ways in which these experiences could impact both his approach toward education and his future legal career.

Although Fiveson's overall tone in this essay is more explanatory than anecdotal, it is generally appropriate to the way in which he presents himself to the reader. Rather than simply listing off the assets of Harvard Law, he connects them to himself and his life goals in such a way that makes it clear to the reader why he is such a good match for the school. For example, he devotes a large part of his essay to describing how his perspectives on human interaction were shaped through his travels, thus leading to a fundamental change in the way he ultimately views the role of law in society. Such detail in Fiveson's introduction of himself and his personal values creates a tangible portrait of his character and, rather than beating around the bush, allows him to directly address the major reasons for his application to Harvard Law.

Nevertheless, the straightforwardness of Fiveson's tone may not always be an asset. In particular, his introduction is a bit dry and too abstract to be relatable to his life experiences and "personal statement." Rather than introducing his essay with a grandiose and rather verbose explanation of law, he should have explored a more personal touch, especially considering his focus on his travels later on in the essay.

But the drier portions of the early paragraphs still demonstrate a capacity for careful reasoning. The references to his international experience are not so much bragging points as they are jumping-off points for a discerning discussion of the law and need for lawyers like the one Fiveson hopes to become.

—*Rebecca Hu*

YONATAN LEVY

"People hearing without listening." These words, immortalized in the Paul Simon and Art Garfunkel song "The Sound of Silence," highlight an important distinction in the human condition, that hearing and listening are not one and the same. Yet both hearing and listening have affected my life in a profound way. While almost everyone has at some point heard a parent, teacher, or girlfriend complain about the difference between the two, I have come to understand it firsthand. I have come to appreciate that while hearing can motivate, it can also frustrate and upset. Listening, on the other hand, can be among the most empowering experiences.

Prior to starting college, I opted for a year of seminary study in Israel. I chose Birkat Moshe in the city of Ma'aleh Adumim because it offered an intensive and immersive program. As one of the top seminaries in Israel with over three hundred Israeli students and only three or four Americans, I expected to be intellectually challenged as well as culturally immersed. The language transition would not be arduous as I already spoke Hebrew fluently, but I was anticipating an exciting period of cultural acclimation.

And acclimate I did. I learned to walk the walk and talk the talk. Yet something gnawed at me. The entire year living in this Middle Eastern country, I would hear the Muslim call to prayer sounding from the minarets. I was overcome by the sounds of Arabic flowing through the *shuk*, the marketplace, yet I could not understand the words being spoken. I knew that if I was going to truly understand the region, I was going to have to take a more active interest in the Arabic culture. After all, as I walked through the streets of Jerusalem, I was certain to hear as much Arabic as Hebrew.

Surprisingly, the more closely I looked at Arabic culture, the more I saw commonality with my own Israeli heritage. I even found connections with my American legacy. After all, we are all people with similar hopes and desires. I was at a loss now to understand the current tensions in the Middle East. How had two such similar peoples grown so far apart?

Perhaps this gap was a result of the distinction between hearing and listening. In college and in my year in Israel, I frequented forums on topics ranging from Jerusalem and the peace process in the Middle East to bridging the gap between the West and the Arab world. I witnessed firsthand the effects of people hearing without listening. Each side listened to its own voices but only merely heard what the other side said. This breach could only be exacerbated by the inability of the two sides to understand each other's language.

When I arrived at college, I embraced the opportunity to study Arabic. I shifted my class schedule to be based around Arabic classes. To my surprise, the more I learned and the more time I spent with my Arab friends the more I found in common with them. My understanding of the language and culture affected my perspective on the people and ultimately the political landscape of the region. To this day, however, even my closest friends do not understand my new perspective. They can't fathom how it came to be, that while they hang out with Ben Goldberg from New York and Daniel Schwartz from Israel, I am hanging out with Ra'if Abdul-Rahman from Saudi Arabia and Mehera Abdelaziz from Lebanon. They are confused that an Orthodox Jewish boy has just as many friends at the Gaza demonstrations on campus as at the Israeli *shuk* day. They are at a loss to understand how I learn about *Yerushalayim Hakdosha* in Jewish Studies classes, while learning about *Al-Quds Al-Karim* in my Arabic classes ("The Holy City of Jerusalem" in Hebrew and Arabic, respectively).

In truth, I have surprised even myself with the close friendships that I have formed with my Arabic classmates. In a sense, however, this surprise was somewhat unwarranted. I'm not saying that it was an easy transition, but I did not have to renounce one culture to begin to accept another. I adopted a new sensitivity, as the phrase "I disagree, but you have the right to your opinion" entered into my daily discourse. I learned when to speak and when not to. Most importantly, I learned how to listen.

My journey toward Arabic really began with hearing years ago in Israel and has led to me listening today. Now as I take the next step in my academic studies, I ask myself what I have taken out of these experiences and how I will apply them to my future endeavors. I have learned the power of listening. My willingness to exercise these new listening skills has yielded amazing results. I plan to pursue a degree in law at Harvard and hope to master the art of persuasion. Now that I have learned to appreciate the power of listening, I would like to learn to construct valid arguments and to deconstruct faulty ones, in the hope that maybe someday I will have others not just hearing me, but truly listening.

Analysis

Have you ever met an Orthodox Jew who majored in Arabic? Me neither. Consequently, it was not only interesting for the reader to learn about Yonatan Levy's unique background, but it was also advantageous for him to capitalize on it in a sea of many qualified law school applicants.

In the first sentence of the essay, Levy uses a well-known song lyric as a keystone for the subsequent theme that develops regarding the dichotomy between listening and hearing. Although a risky approach because initial quotations can sometimes overshadow the words of the candidate himself, it pays off nicely for Levy, whose mature and concise writing style supports the complex nature of his subject.

Additionally, the candidate draws from an unconventional year abroad, a seminar study in Israel where his first encounter of the mix between Middle Eastern Jews and Muslims unfolds. As he continues on, explaining his motivation behind studying Arabic and forming connections between the two peoples in terms of their cultures and American legacy, he uses a mixture of personal experience and metaphor to demonstrate his unique background and diversity. Although the study abroad is simply listed in Levy's résumé, the reader now has a taste of what it truly entailed. Most importantly, he refers back to his listening versus hearing theme when discussing the forums he attended by the Palestine and Israel societies in college.

Once again, Levy repeatedly emphasizes his bridging perspective and the confusion of others as to why he engages with both cultures so intensively, providing examples of his seemingly opposite friends and their reactions when finding about the existence of the other. This reads nicely and can serve as an example for descriptive storytelling. To Levy's credit, the perspective is valuable, and his personal growth and recognition that the two cultures can exist simultaneously within him allows for some humility.

Finally, Levy ends with the listening and hearing theme once again, but with a twist. As a self-proclaimed listener, he switches to a desire to persuade, both of which are skills required of a lawyer. He concisely offers a reason as to why he would be a good lawyer and why he wants to be a lawyer in the first place, thereby specializing the essay for its purpose.

—Amna Hashmi

INSPIRATION

Why do you want to be a lawyer? For some applicants, that's been obvious since birth. For others, it's a midlife reversal after years spent doing something very distant from law. Inspiration can come in the form of a person or a cause or even everyday life.

Writing an essay about your inspiration, though, isn't the same thing as spelling out, "I want to be a lawyer because . . ." complete with three supporting arguments. Instead, you'll notice that the strongest essays in this section fuse observation, experience, and reflection into a subtler proof of motivation. And that core motivation varies widely. For one writer, inspiration is a battle with homelessness. For another, it is the cause of animal rights. For another, it is witnessing the realities of life in the U.S. capital.

Like all good personal statements, these essays combine a number of techniques and approaches. They bend narratives of growth and evolution into law school inspiration, which doesn't require a single eureka moment. They reason through and reflect on the broader societal issues that spur law school interest. Many of the most effective answer the questions "Who are you?" and "Why law school?" simultaneously. The stories of your identity, growth, and commitment will naturally interweave. Let your essay show that.

MICHAEL JACOBSON

I always thought my inspiration to attend law school would come from my time in the courtroom. I never could have guessed it would come from the backseat of a police cruiser.

Mock trial has been a major part of my life ever since high school. While many of my classmates avoided class presentations or speaking opportunities, I have always relished the challenge of captivating an audience. It never mattered if I was delivering a thirty-minute campus tour or a thirty-second tenor saxophone solo over a Coltrane tune; I found the pressure to perform in front of an audience both nerve-racking and exhilarating. Nothing was more exciting, however, than entering a courtroom, standing before a judge, and setting the tone of a three-hour case with my opening statement for the prosecution.

The first thing I did after moving into my dorm at Georgetown University freshman year was to sign up to try out for the mock trial team. From day one I enjoyed giving opening statements and playing the part of a witness, giving me the opportunity to become a more polished public speaker, to learn more about the Federal Rules of Evidence, and to experiment with my acting abilities.

Mock trial soon became my favorite (and busiest) extracurricular activity. I loved the challenges of leading the team as captain and working with and learning from a group of brilliant and ambitious freshmen and sophomores. I found an opportunity to teach both public speaking and mock trial over the summer in Washington, D.C., and my love of the mock courtroom only continued to increase through sophomore year. This inspired me to pursue an internship at the U.S. Attorney's Office (USAO) in Washington, D.C. All spring I looked forward to seeing my world of make-believe law come to life.

I was sitting in the back of a squad car: sweating, overdressed, and firmly out of my element. The D.C. version of Tubbs and Crockett sat up front, speeding down the dark alleyways of southeast D.C. Before I could catch my breath, the man who had just committed a hit-and-run was in handcuffs and I found myself in a rare state of speechlessness.

After taking part in the arrest, I was able to follow this case, along with a handful of others, to its conclusion throughout the summer. It was a great way to get to know some amazing attorneys and law students. Furthermore, I enjoyed learning about the criminal legal process.

What stuck with me the most from my summer at USAO, surprisingly, wasn't flashing lights, bright courtrooms, or compelling oral arguments. It was the hit-and-run victim, a tiny woman with her arm cut to the bone, keeping her head held high throughout the interview. It was the strength she showed during the most difficult time in her life that still resonates and inspires me to this day.

I learned a lot about the criminal legal process that summer. But what was most valuable was the human element that comes with being a prosecutor. Don't get me wrong; I still solo in the jazz band and grab every opportunity to debate or present in class. I still love giving campus tours. And I still give opening statements in mock trial. But it took a ride in a squad car and seeing firsthand how an attorney can positively change a life to truly understand why I want to pursue a legal education.

Analysis

Michael Jacobson's essay traces his development from a mock trial competitor in high school and college to an intern in the D.C. Attorney's Office, to a Harvard Law School applicant. Jaconbson's interest in law is twofold. On the one hand, he enjoys the role of lawyer, the analysis and the presentation he has appreciated since his early days. Despite this constant, the essay is a story of change, too. Jacobson explains how his almost instinctive interest in the law intersects with a newfound, more conceptual interest, an interest spurred by the likes of the hit-and-run victim. He gives the reader a window into how he has matured.

There are a few loose ends in Jacobson's essay, though. For example, it is rather unclear how his various inspirations—riding in the back of a police car (first paragraph), a victim's strength (seventh paragraph), or the positive impact of an attorney (last paragraph)—relate together in forming an inspiration. And they are presented in absolute terms—"nothing was more exciting" than being in front of a courtroom, the victim "stuck with me the most," and yet the backseat of a squad car was the most influential moment. However, in spite of a few instances of hyperbole, Jacobson's essay showcases his experience and achievements excellently.

The essay's content is its greatest asset. It is personal; the reader feels like he or she knows Jacobson. He integrates his experience with mock trial, his enjoyment of speaking and presenting, and his awareness of both the human and professional aspects of law. The essay is a little rough around the edges, but the narrative structure is a good window into Jacobson's life, and, most importantly, the essay communicates his ambition and experience.

—Eliza Hale

STEPHEN IYA

As a child I would often stand in the corridor staring at an old portrait of my mother. I was perplexed not by her youth, but by her stern demeanor and strange attire. In the picture, she wore a black gown and a white collaret connected to two linen bands. What puzzled me the most, however, was the ridiculous wig she wore. Curly, white, and garish, the wig stole the limelight of the picture and in my mind, this is what a lawyer looked like—pompous, intimidating, and ostentatious. Oddly, I found this portrait to be both alienating and alluring. Though it depicted a representation of my mother I was not familiar with, it somehow drew me in. I knew that before immigrating to the United States, my mother had served as a lawyer in the Nigerian government. She had since explained to me that as a barrister and solicitor of the Supreme Court of Nigeria she was required to wear the ornate attire I had seen in the picture. And although I knew her to be humble, personable, and quite effervescent, I associated her days as an attorney with the picture on the wall and was strangely drawn to the confidence and power it represented.

Growing up, I assumed the woman in the portrait represented my mother's past life, one she had left behind after coming to America. As a young mother and an immigrant to America, it had been difficult for her to find the time or money to pursue a legal career in the United States. Instead, she decided to become a licensed practical nurse. Though I constantly caught her flipping through books on U.S. law and engaging in intense conversations with other attorneys in her free time, she divided most of her time between raising children and tending to parental home patients. From her I discovered I, too, gained a sense of fulfillment from investing time and effort into people and I decided the most effective way to continue to do so was to join the medical profession.

As I progressed through my undergraduate years, I soon realized that medicine was not my passion. Uncertain about what I wanted to do with my life, I threw myself into a myriad of campus activities. I helped teach English to Latino immigrants, served as a resident adviser in my dorm, and coached students on how to best represent themselves to prospective employers. What I learned from my activities was that I wasn't satisfied with just helping people; I gained my energy by working with people and assisting them in realizing their potential and overcoming their issues. I decided to study public policy because I was perturbed by the disconnect between one's legal rights and his or her actual capabilities. I sought to understand how laws and policies could be better translated into real, tangible change. As a public policy major, I learned that I was intrigued about the legal system and how it protects human rights and provides for social justice.

Although I knew I was interested in the legal system, I finally realized that a legal education would enable me to live out my passions while I was at home overhearing a conversation my mother was having with a Caribbean immigrant who had just lost her baby. As my mother listened to the woman's story, she began to discern that this was most likely a case of malpractice. Though the woman was completely ignorant of both medical standards and her legal rights, she was able to pursue justice because my mother had been trained in this arena and was willing to help. Without my mother's help, the woman would have lacked the knowledge and resources to translate her legally defined rights into actual capabilities. As I began to recall the countless times my mother had drawn upon her legal background, I began to comprehend that she was constantly drawing upon her legal education to provide practical assistance to others in need. I now understand that though my mother has since "taken off the wig" she continues to be a woman of power, confidence, and influence as she sacrifices her time off the job to assist people in better realizing their rights.

Though I once associated the legal profession with ostentation, stringency, and dominance, I have come to associate it with the humility, compassion, and sacrifice I watched my mother exhibit. While I am still drawn to the influence and the agency of the legal profession, I have come to the realization that there is power in selflessness and that these qualities can be used to empower others.

I have since realized that the life of a lawyer, and of a law school student, is by no means easy and that in order to endure the long hours and sleepless nights, there must be some motivating factor. Not only have I discovered that the subject of law intrigues me, but I have also experienced how rewarding it is to help people realize their dreams—whether they be to speak English, to land a job, or to find justice. I am confident that I will succeed in law school because I know the legal profession will help me realize my own passion, and in my experiences, it has been difficult to fail where fulfillment is found.

Analysis

The essay's opening is an invitation. Stephen Iya shares his conception of his mother with the reader, helping us to see the image he once saw and, by extension, to understand the broader points he goes on to make. From this point forward, he effectively uses this initial anecdote as a lens through which he explains his path toward discovering that the legal field was the right area for him.

Iya's essay follows his own coming-of-age and realization that the legal world was the one he belonged to. While he follows the initial anecdote in a chronological order, the quantity of life phases that he describes limits each portion's quality. It is important to keep in mind that as you devote many portions of your personal statement to many different events or anecdotes, that you will be limiting the detail you can include for each part. In Iya's essay, this limited detail for some portions of his essay leads to a read that at times seems as if he is simply telling his readers different things, instead of demonstrating how he came to such realizations with greater detail.

Although Iya's mother played a major role in his understanding of the legal system and its ability to let him live out his passions, at times the essay seems to be dominated by facts about his mother, and less about himself. These essays are an opportunity to convey as much about *you* as possible to the readers, so although describing relationships and interactions with others can be an effective means to convey a point, the primary focus should clearly be the product of the relationships.

When investing a great portion of the essay to a single anecdote, as Iya does with the first paragraph in his essay, it's important to tie the other portions of the essay to the same anecdote, allowing the story to become whole. Iya demonstrates this well as his story comes full circle in his last few paragraphs; drawing in elements from the portrait of his mother he began with to tie off a successful essay.

—*Zohra Yaqhubi*

EMMA RAVIV

The smile on Byron Halsey's face on July 9, 2007, was the widest I'd ever seen. Standing on the marble front steps of the Elizabeth, New Jersey, courthouse in which he'd just sat, for what he hoped was the last time, he looked up at the sky and inhaled deeply. "How do you feel?" "I'm free," he breathed into the brandished TV microphone, relieved.

About an hour earlier, I had been perched on an unforgiving wooden bench in a relatively unadorned hall in the courthouse, holding a sign in my hands that read, FREE BYRON HALSEY. A stack of them was being distributed; he had fans, apparently. That day, and forevermore, I would count myself among them.

Mr. Halsey had already been free, by most accounts, for a number of months. DNA evidence having released him previously from prison, he was in Elizabeth that day for a formality—the legal exoneration. The State admitting that it was wrong. A big "oops," though remarkably, no "I'm sorry." He had been in jail for nineteen years—my entire life, at the time—for the horrific murders of two children, murders he did not commit.

I don't know what it is about this stuff that so shocks me, so shakes me by the shoulders. Maybe it's that my faith in something has been taken from me. Maybe it's that I feel for the victims of these crimes' botched proceedings, or that I could so closely observe the palpable shame and sheepishness on the part of the judges, the mistaken prosecutors, and the misled eyewitnesses. Or maybe, just maybe, it's this: I feel I can do something about it.

So many things in life that are hard or wrong, I cannot change. I cannot affect in any way the human inability to fly or to teleport or to travel back in time. I cannot affect in any real way the economy here or the economic disparity in other countries. I cannot cure AIDS or cancer, and I am helplessly unable to stop whalers, poachers, or murderers.

This, though, I can change. I saw the Innocence Project attorneys litigate on Mr. Halsey's behalf, and I saw the raw gratitude he felt. Indeed, I saw the difference just one person's work could make. In Byron Halsey's smile that day, I found my cause.

I have always believed in the following-your-dreams thing, but I can't say I've stumbled upon many ideas that have grabbed me, or not more than other general interests like grammar, whale saving, and poetry—things I can continue to care about. Certainly, I was not like my childhood best friend who "needed" to be a vet, and then an astronaut, and then a ballerina. I was always envious of that passion back then, but now I know why I did not have it: My cause came later.

And I'm glad it did. I'm glad I found it at the age of action, the classic age of decision making. I'm glad I was old enough to acquire an internship with the Innocence Project in New York that summer, and I'm glad I can continue to fight for this cause two years later in the Washington, D.C., office. As an undergraduate, I do what I can—I contacted and created literature for donors in 2007, and I now serve as the primary screener for potentially innocent prisoners' letters, investigating fifteen-year-old murder cases on the side. I skim the surface, but am structurally unable to delve much deeper. As I'm well aware, one needs a law degree for that.

All that brings me here. I'm on the brink of the next enormous step in pursuing this cause, and Harvard Law School has everything I need, and could ever want, to make that leap. A startlingly accomplished faculty coupled with the most clinical opportunities of any law school in the country will propel me to join the fight with the credentials that allow me to truly do so.

In the stifling heat outside that courtroom, before cameras, crying family members, and legal professionals, I found my place. In countless other harrowing stories of exonerees, I found my inspiration. And in the Harvard classroom, I believe I can find the knowledge, and thus the power, to make my cause a reality.

Analysis

In retelling the prisoner's story, Emma Raviv simultaneously narrates the history of her burgeoning interest in law and her vicarious experience of liberation through the released prisoner. Raviv is effective in her essay because her detailed personal experience convincingly demonstrates her motivations for attending law school via her story. Throughout the entire essay, she artfully builds upon the story of the prisoner to illustrate her activism and how her career and personal aspirations necessitate a law degree.

What stands out about Raviv's essay is her candid and unpretentious voice through which she articulates her genuine interest in law. The fourth paragraph is one of her strongest, as she expresses how her own emotional reaction to the prisoner's story has fueled her passion for law. She demonstrates her ongoing commitment to her cause by describing her qualifications and subsequent internship with the Innocence Project and work screening prisoners' letter, demonstrating ongoing commitment to her cause. Her passion for social justice is clear, showing the admissions officers that she has identified a specific pathway within law to pursue.

Raviv utilizes the last few paragraphs to convey why her attendance at law school is so necessary and urgent, relaying that she has done everything she can without a law degree, but is "structurally unable to delve much deeper." Although she compellingly explains how a Harvard law degree will give her the credentials to "make that leap," parts of Raviv's second-to-last paragraph may be perceived as excessive flattery; indeed, she seems overconfident that HLS "has everything [she] need[s]," and certainly the admissions committee is already aware of the "startlingly accomplished faculty."

Raviv's conclusion ties together her essay nicely, revisiting the court scene from the introduction and reflecting on her personal discoveries since then. In an eloquent last sentence, Raviv makes a final push to the admissions officers, indicating that Harvard will empower her to "make [her] cause a reality." Overall, Raviv successfully convinces the reader that law school is the perfect fit for her, given her interests and experiences.

—*Michelle S. Lee*

ANONYMOUS

"What is wrong with you!? These men are killers! They kill for a living, it's only a matter of time before one of them snaps. You'll be next." This sentiment, echoed many times by loved ones, was not enough to dissuade me from doing the last thing anyone in my family could have predicted.

I have seen more tears since I began working on Fort Bragg six months ago than in the whole of my twenty-four years. I saw tears of joy as I handed over the keys to a newlywed couple's first home. I saw tears of relief as I explained our insurance policy to a family who had lost everything in a fire. I saw tears of frustration as I strove for objectivity while investigating charges of spousal abuse. I saw tears of helplessness as I struggled to help a mother who could not afford to feed her children while supporting her drug habit. The most distressing are tears that I can do nothing to assuage, the tears of those who have just discovered the person they have been waiting for will not return from their last deployment. While my formal education gave me the framework to understand international conflict at an abstract level, my experiences since graduation have shown me the importance of that research.

My background is drastically different from that of my coworkers: I am neither a veteran, nor an army brat, nor an army wife. I accepted this position with the goal of working toward positive change, but with no idea how the experience would change me. To do my job I had to become fluent in the language of the military and overcome a culture shock greater than any I experienced living abroad. I pass through two armed checkpoints on my daily commute, entering an environment completely alien to everything I knew before. Until a few years ago I had never met a soldier, had never held a gun, had never contemplated the questions that arise when a single decision literally determines life or death. Much has changed since then.

Growing up and attending college in the birthplace of the free speech movement, I was no stranger to alternative lifestyles and attitudes. After 9/11, when most of the country discovered its patriotism, the youth of Berkeley embraced a stark antiwar stance. NO BLOOD FOR OIL stickers plastered the hallways of my high school, as well as my own books. My interest in international conflict was born during rallies that drew me out of class to march down the streets, carried along in a surging mob. I found comfort in a collective naïveté, invariably coupled with the heartfelt belief that we could change the world by protesting the epitome of evil: war. However, as I began to study politics I found the attitude of "us" versus "them" a gross oversimplification. I wanted to effect change, not simply voice my grievances. I spent my college career searching for clarification, but my research only exposed deeper questions. I had the intellectual framework to understand the reasons behind conflict, but found myself lost in applying this knowledge toward a palpable goal.

The basic difference between my own understanding of the world and that of my peers was exposed when my involvement with the military struck an ideological nerve. During my senior year, I met and formed close friendships with a platoon of airborne infantrymen returning from the front lines of Afghanistan. Witnessing firsthand the manifestations of post-traumatic stress disorder, listening to the ideological debates that raged among them, and watching personal camera clips that would never be aired to the public, I discovered the fundamental aspect of my studies. Directly confronted with their shared memories, I finally understood the human cost of war. The extreme difference between what they had lived through and my neat understanding of conflict put everything I had learned into perspective and inspired me to use my education to serve in my own way. After graduation, in an effort to further understand the system I was intent on improving, I immersed myself in a military community.

Although I lost lifelong friendships for empathizing with "killers," I moved to the largest military base in the conservative South with the aim of contributing in a concrete way. I was hired by the military housing office and have since been a counselor, advocate, and friend to countless people I would otherwise never have met. Every positive effect I have had on someone else's life has inspired me to continue with the goal of eventually doing so on a larger scale. By pursuing a legal career, I believe I can increase my contribution from the personal to the farther-reaching, tangible policy level. It only takes one victory to set a precedent.

Despite a pause in my formal education, I spent the last year learning some of life's most important and profound lessons. I now know a deeper strength within myself I would never have discovered had I not thrust myself into a new environment, where the most life-changing events are daily occurrences. I am confident this strength will sustain me in my continued efforts to serve my community.

Analysis

The author doesn't simply offer an interesting experience. She explains how her experience is situated in the broader narrative of her own personal development. And she also does so in a way that fully engages the reader word by word.

One of the best assets of the essay is its ample supply of vivid, tangible imagery and examples. With every assertion that she makes, the author supports the claim with multiple experiences and interactions that she encountered during her time at Fort Bragg, a U.S. Army installation. From her high school years to the present, she details every feeling and every emotion so that the reader can step into her shoes and live the world through her eyes. Her prose flows so smoothly that it mimics the style of a vignette or a story, rather than that of an academic essay.

However, despite the unique and extremely intriguing nature of her writing style, the essay does fail to adequately connect the incredible stories and life experiences to the author's own personal goals and values. In fact, the essay first mentions her desire to pursue a legal career only in the last sentence of the penultimate paragraph, leaving little space to actually address the prompt in comparison to the effort devoted to detailing her actual experiences. This structure may also prove to be difficult for the reader to understand, and it's easy to get lost in the sea of memories and stories. As the goal of the essay is to most effectively reflect personal character and goals, the author could more effectively convey her message by leaving more room to ultimately relate her amazing stories and encounters to her present-day goal and perspective on life.

The essay's strengths are considerable, though. Some experiences help us learn by encountering and observing others. Other experiences challenge us, and we learn through adversity. The author's story encompasses both. Her meshing of the people she has met with the person she has, in spite of challenges, become makes for a truly personal statement.

—*Rebecca Hu*

ANGELA CHAN

After a sleep-depriving round of midterms in our study abroad courses at the University of Cambridge, a friend and I finally embark on our long-awaited visit to Italy. Rome, with its stone fountains and age-old monuments, promises to hold all the romantic nostalgia worthy of its title as the Eternal City. Within the first minutes of our arrival, however, disaster strikes. A pickpocket steals all of my friend's cash, credit cards, and IDs, and suddenly we are no longer young adults chasing a childhood dream, but victims of a crime in a country whose language we cannot speak. Despite our efforts, her wallet is not recovered; even the police can only offer a belated warning of caution.

Still visibly shaken, my friend mourns the injustice more than the theft: How can anyone commit an act so morally wrong, especially when it only hurts innocent bystanders? Though I understand her indignation, I cannot help but quietly wonder if anyone truly steals for the sake of immorality. Not only in Rome, but also in Paris, Barcelona, and the other major cities we travel to, there is an unexpected and underlying presence of poverty. While tourists spend the equivalent of $20 on Italian gelato, children beg for pennies beside the Pantheon. Even my economics classes cannot prepare me for such striking illustrations of the uneven distribution of wealth. It is true, there is injustice here—but in a world of excess, it seems the real victims are those who do not even have enough to live by.

I lead a more than privileged life: I have a loving, supportive family, a God-given penchant for learning, and enough financial stability to pursue even personal interests like the performing arts. These are blessings my term abroad has taught me not to take for granted. There are so many less fortunate than I, I who did nothing to deserve being born where and who I am, with the possibility and ability to achieve my dreams. This is not a shortsighted epiphany, quickly dispelled by the concerns of everyday life, but a conviction that inspires me to use my opportunities to achieve more; the American dream, for me, is a universal one. Never again do

I want to feel like I did that semester, limited to an apologetic smile and a few euros in an empty cup, helpless to help those whom my heart broke for. No, I with all my privileges, with my U.S. citizenship, education, socioeconomic foundation, and bicultural understanding, am in such a prime position to impact the lives of others, to alleviate burdens, and create lasting improvements—and I have no intention of doing any less.

With the mind-set that I needed to start somewhere, no matter how small, I returned home to pursue an internship with Kaiser Permanente, the nation's largest nonprofit health plan. I could not imagine a place better suited to teach me the ways of helping others, and they did not disappoint: Day in and day out, I rectified pain points caused by misleading information on our website and ensured customer service agents were equipped with the most accurate responses. My work contributed to productive and medically sound interactions with Kaiser's online services, delivering a safe patient experience to the over four million members who utilized our digital properties. Now this, this was real change, and I was confident it would only lead to even greater ones. Despite all my excitement at the positive impact I was making, however, I soon saw that even the end of this road was not enough for me. Numerous times, the problems I worked on were elevated to the legal staff because the roots of the issues lay in the law, not the execution. Only the lawyers were equipped to protect the patient as well as the health plan, thus allowing Kaiser to continue serving many more. Their influence was not confined to the boardroom either; both distraught mothers and furious grandsons, all moved by concern for a loved one's well-being, were calmed by the professionalism and efficiency with which our lawyers resolved their cases. With such personal interaction coupled with the ability to address and remedy real-life concerns, law seemed to be the epitome of all that I sought for.

My experience at Kaiser Permanente has shown me several ways to address the needs of a community; my memories of studying abroad urge me to find my greatest capacity to do so. I choose law school because I have seen firsthand the greater reach of such an education. I will not allow a lack of knowledge or dedication, factors that I can affect, to hinder me from giving to my fullest extent. Legal training will also hone my unique skills and interests, increasing upon my greatest strengths so that I can best serve others. And I know that it is broad and idealistic, this goal of "helping others," but the lack of specificity doesn't make the pain I feel at seeing another's suffering or their suffering itself any less real. With time, I will better define how exactly I can be of use to my community. Law school is the first step in that direction, ensuring that I will be more than ready to act upon it when I do, and to do so to my greatest potential.

Analysis

The real strength in this essay is its sincerity. One genuinely believes that Angela Chan wishes to go to law school in order to help others. Giving an example of how to apply a law degree after school is obviously important to include, but in this example it is further strengthened by the entire structure of the piece. Although the Kaiser example alone would have been a reason to apply to law school, the description of her experience in Italy allows us to catch a glimpse of who she is and where her moral judgment comes from—both very important takeaways from a personal statement. Chan effectively prefaces how she hopes to help others by first providing background on why she wishes to help them in the first place. She also brings the study abroad experience back at the end, which makes the example feel more grounded.

Another aspect that lends itself to a note of sincerity is her voice in the piece. With stylistic choices like, "Now this, this was real change . . ." we can see that Chan is not simply putting on airs but is speaking as passionately and fluidly in her essay as she would in person. She does little to glamorize the settings in which she finds herself—Italy and in the workplace at Kaiser—but rather very clearly depicts problems that she encountered and how she tried to remedy them. She conveys her sense of both enjoyment in helping others and dissatisfaction in not being able to do more. I did feel that some of her statements were a bit vague and/or grandiose, such as, "I could not imagine a place better suited to teach me the ways of helping others," but because she acknowledges her goals as "broad and idealistic" this didn't detract too much from her argument.

Finally, this essay has a great tone of humility. Although talking about one's accomplishments is unavoidable in any application, Chan does so by talking about the privilege she has in being able to help others. This sense of gratitude is refreshing and appealing of any candidate, especially when coupled with a clear desire to be proactive and take advantage of opportunities. Chan manages to shows us what she hopes to do with a law degree without being overly righteous.

—Anneli Tostar

JAMES BAKER JR.

Dusk had begun to edge its way across the parking lot, and up to our dented minivan. I leaned against the door until the side of my face pressed against the window, hoping to maximize the remaining light. Squinting, I lifted my notepad only inches from my face, careful to balance the calculator on one knee. The cars and trucks that earlier filled the truck stop were dwindling. For a moment, I lost track of what I was doing and gazed at the families scurrying to the restrooms and back. For just another moment, I wondered what sort of homes they would return to, what they looked and sounded like. Flickering streetlamps quickly brought back my focus, however, and I anxiously tried to speed up my calculations. It was late. The sun was setting. Without the daylight I would never finish my homework.

I heard my mom in the front seat mention something, but I was too caught up in the problems to comprehend much else. Only one page to go and I was confident that, like many nights before, I would finish just in time. She repeated, "Are you hungry?" She spoke without looking up. She rarely did when she asked *that* question.

"No thanks, I'm fine," I assured her, though the pangs in my stomach were becoming more pronounced. "I'm still good from the school lunch. You have enough to grab something for yourself?"

My mom quickly mumbled, "I'm okay, too. I had something at work." I ignored her equally false assurance; my thoughts were completely on my homework. The sun was about to dip under the horizon and I had to finish. . . .

For as long as I've been pursuing an education, I've found ways to succeed under tumultuous, often inadequate, living conditions. My elementary school years were spent zigzagging from school district to school district throughout California's Bay Area and Central Valley, in my family's search for work and shelter. I completed middle school and my freshman year of high school in an independent study program with six teachers for several hundred students. By tenth grade, I had already spent more than a decade surviving in motels, cars, spare rooms, and a Salvation Army shelter.

Yet, neither my parents nor I allowed our struggle with home-lessness to excuse mediocrity. Not that I sought an excuse. No matter what situation I was in, I pursued my education relentlessly. My studies sheltered my developing mind and nurtured my insatia-ble curiosity. They provided an outlet for the competitiveness, cre-ativity, and energy that my family's hardships suppressed. I initially saw education as a respite from the everyday stresses of poverty. But, as I matured, I've come to realize that education was, undoubt-edly, the best, if not the only way to truly and permanently change my station in life. My passion for education helped me win a schol-arship that enabled me to be the first member of my extended fam-ily to attend college.

I recognize that I am an exception, however, and that far too many students are denied the opportunities that I had, opportuni-ties that are critical to economic and social stability. In college, I lobbied my state's legislators to invest in outreach programs for underrepresented students, tutored hundreds of remedial students and English learners, and served as a mock trial coach for incom-ing Equal Opportunity Program freshmen. While I benefited from working directly with disadvantaged students, I sought a deeper and broader understanding of some of the gravest educational chal-lenges facing so many of America's youth. This goal eventually led me to Washington, D.C., where I interned for the U.S. Senate HELP Committee, in the late Edward M. Kennedy's education policy of-fice. There, I not only researched education policy, but, just as im-portantly, witnessed the dynamics surrounding its formation.

Last summer, my pursuit of education led me to the TRIALS program at Harvard Law School where I enjoyed an experience usually available only to HLS students, studying law with Harvard professors. During a mock class, Professor Ronald Sullivan Jr. played devil's advocate as I tried to enunciate the challenges in inter-preting the ruling in *Terry v. Ohio*. In improvising an indignant, un-cooperative delinquent while I acted as her patient, yet, persistent counsel, Professor Gloria Tan demonstrated the daily challenges public defenders face. The weeks I spent learning among students and faculty reaffirmed and deepened my desire to pursue a legal education. My goal of using the law as a tool to enact social change has never seemed more attainable.

From my seat in a chilly van at an isolated truck stop, I once thought I lacked the light needed to finish my work. I now know differently. Education has always been my light, though my work remains unfinished. A Harvard legal education will enable me to partake in a public service career, through which I can shape policy and help cast education's light over any child who seeks it.

Analysis

Admissions officers are looking for students who are not only talented, but who also understand and articulate why exactly they want to attend the school. Extreme or abject life circumstances are neither necessary nor sufficient to secure admission, but James Baker Jr.'s essay shines because it carefully connects his difficult upbringing and his hope to enact social change in the realm of education with his desire to spend three years at Harvard Law School.

The statement is strong from the beginning. In the opening paragraphs, Baker uses an anecdote to establish for the admissions committee that although his childhood was chaotic and replete with hardship, "neither my parents nor I allowed our struggle with homelessness to excuse mediocrity." Baker's perseverance—he explains how he earned a scholarship to college and became the first in his family to attend—is indeed impressive all on its own. Perhaps more compelling, though, is that Baker speaks of committing himself to changing the equation and increasing access and opportunity for those who grow up under difficult circumstances. In a move that makes his outlook all the more impressive, he portrays himself—the child who grew up in homeless poverty—as the lucky one. "[F]ar too many students are denied the opportunities that I had," he says, and goes on to carry that sentiment forward to his work for equal opportunity. Baker demonstrates how a personal statement's tone and attitude can say as much as its more concrete information and details.

Moreover, his stated desire to help others is bolstered by relevant experience in the field, including work on Capitol Hill and at a summer program at HLS. And while impressive experiences in a chosen field of study or interest are not prerequisites for admission to a school like Harvard Law, they can be helpful if articulated and incorporated well into a larger argument, as Baker does here.

The essay ends with a strong conclusion, which brings the reader back to the opening imagery of Baker's difficult upbringing, and restates his commitment to working for those who are under-privileged in access and opportunity. His final sentence is a summation of his entire argument, representing a compelling case for admission.

—*Matt Clarida*

JASON LEE

During my final months at Stanford University, I received the same well-intentioned advice from many different people: Don't pick a job for money or prestige, pick it because it's what you love to do. I was happy to comply. With a lifelong love of performance and two proudly acquired degrees in Drama and Communication, I moved to Los Angeles to pursue a career in the dramatic arts. Never mind that I had never visited the city, that I did not know anyone living there, and that I had not secured employment. As my mother once learned when I was twelve years old, after she tried unsuccessfully to dissuade me from accompanying her on a sixteen-mile hike up Half Dome mountain in Yosemite National Park: When I set my mind to doing something, I do it.

I steadfastly pursued my artistic aspirations for four years until a news bulletin on June 2, 2008, diverted my attention away from Hollywood and toward Sacramento. In cold, sober tones, our California Attorney General announced that the ballot initiative Proposition 8 had officially qualified for our November election. Aimed at eliminating the right to marry for gays and lesbians, Prop 8 was a clear indication that my home state was the next great battleground in the marriage equality movement. I had never thought of myself as an overtly political person and had no prior experience working for a political cause, yet I disagreed so strongly with the principles embodied in Prop 8 that I immediately decided to join those fighting on the front lines of this struggle.

My first shift took place at a Beverly Hills voter call center with twenty other nervous volunteers. As we shared our reasons for getting involved, I felt proud that so many people from different backgrounds had come together to support the campaign. We had gays defending their newfound right to marry and straight allies fighting on behalf of friends, siblings, and coworkers. We had Caucasians, African Americans, Asians, and Latinos of varying ages and religions. The fact that our modest voter call center had brought together such a diverse group of people, all united in a desire to protect the rights of an embattled minority, filled me with optimism.

I dedicated myself to the campaign over the next four months, working shifts across Los Angeles County—from voter outreach at a synagogue in Malibu to volunteer recruitment on the streets of West Hollywood. The campaign's pace was exhausting, but the encouragement we received from our supporters always energized me. My most memorable instance of this took place after a late-night volunteer shift when some friends and I retired to a bar to unwind. We struck up a conversation with a woman visiting from Texas who, upon learning that we worked for the No on Prop 8 campaign, told us, "You guys are so lucky to be gay right now—you get to transform the world. You won't just be recipients of change, you get to make it happen." It was such a beautiful message. When I felt discouraged or despondent during the campaign's final weeks, I thought back on that conversation and reaffirmed my commitment to our cause.

In the end, our efforts were insufficient to sway the state electorate to our side and Prop 8 passed by a slim 4 percent margin. Though the voters have made their decision, I definitely do not feel like my work is done—I didn't stop campaigning when I met a voter that I couldn't convince, and I won't give up simply because an election didn't go our way. The struggle for equality depends upon the participation of those who feel passionate about it, and without a doubt, I am one of those people.

My involvement with the No on Prop 8 campaign has provided a new direction for my life. It has led me to pursue an education in law so that I might make a more significant contribution in future battles for civil rights. Prop 8 was merely the beginning of a life-long commitment to social justice, and I know that a legal education will provide me with a foundation for achieving great success in that arena. This path has not been easy thus far, and I know that it will only get more challenging, but I am determined to see it through. When I set my mind to doing something, I do it. Just ask my mom.

Analysis

In his personal statement, Jason Lee uses a defining personal experience—in his case, his work to support same-sex marriage in California—to provide readers with a lens through which to view his candidacy and his desire to attend Harvard Law School.

This is a popular strategy for admissions essays, and writers who do it well—like Lee—weave their experiences into a compelling narrative that makes a strong case for admission.

The essay begins anecdotally, with Lee telling his readers about his decision to pursue a career in acting after college, and using a story about a long hike to demonstrate a streak of determination. Then, the statement takes a surprising turn, as Lee speaks about being drawn to work on the No on Prop 8 campaign in California. The argument he presents is relatively simple but powerful at the same time: While Proposition 8 passed, Lee has not given up working as an advocate, and he implies that he looks at a Harvard legal education as a tool that will help him in that endeavor.

That the essay shows Lee changing and growing only makes it stronger. The essay opens with Jason Lee the dramatic artist who "had never thought of myself as an overtly political person and had no prior experience working for a political cause." By the end, the reader knows and appreciates Jason Lee the committed activist and law school applicant. The course that connects the two demonstrates the strength of not only Lee's ideals and determination but also his openness to new experiences.

An interesting thread in Lee's essay is his occasional anecdotal reference to his mother. While the reference works in the introduction, it does so in the context of a more substantive narrative, the allusion to his mom, which ends the statement is not as effective. Generally, writers should strive to end their admissions statements with, at the least, summations of their narrative or their case to be admitted.

But what makes Lee's essay especially strong is his choice of topic. By choosing to write about his work on the No on Prop 8 campaign, he has picked an experience that not only demonstrates his commitment to social justice, but also, as he explains later in the statement, represents a moment when his perception changed significantly.

—Matt Clarida

AVERY E. HOOK

This may be where I die. A tsunami is heading toward the coast, we don't know how large it will be or when it will hit, and this daft old woman just made a wrong turn, driving us straight to the water's edge. I'm sure she's a perfectly nice person, but, in this moment, I just barely resist the urge to throw her out of the driver's seat. I'm not panicking, just being realistic: We need to get to higher ground right now. All the stories that the local Samoans have been telling me suddenly flood my mind. By the time you see the "*galulolo*," as they call it, it's already too late. I scan the horizon anyway. When the first tsunami occurred a week ago, the entire harbor at Pago Pago drained as the giant wave sucked out all of the water just before it funneled down the bay and pummeled the coastline. Dozens died in the last tsunami, and hundreds of homes were destroyed. I have assessed many of these homes and heard firsthand the stories of their owners: Wilson, whose niece drowned after the wave pulled her from her mother; Iakopo, whose family barely made it upstairs before the wave crushed the lower story of his house; and Sinatoga, who calmly showed me the site where I would not have otherwise suspected her house once stood. How will the American Samoan people withstand another disaster? Moreover, where are my friends? I came to American Samoa with twenty other AmeriCorps National Civilian Community Corps (NCCC) team leaders, and right now I can only account for two of them. Many are constructing tents in some of the worst hit villages on the western end of the island. Without telephone communication, how will they know to run for their lives?

I am a little embarrassed by some of the thoughts that raced through my head on October 7. We received word that we had an hour to get to higher ground, and, once we arrived at a safe elevation, we were informed that the tsunami warning had been canceled. Never did I expect to flee for my life in a tsunami warning (or do so twice, as I did again on October 19). Nor did I expect to be on a tropical island with the American Red Cross in the first place. Two years ago, I began a series of interviews with an eighty-three-year-old

Holocaust survivor named Ursula. Over the course of several weeks, she told me her life story. She related how her father and brother perished after her family was shipped off to Terezín and then Auschwitz. Ursula survived because two German soldiers took pity on her, disobeyed orders, and dropped her off at a factory en route back to Auschwitz after a stint at a work camp. Ursula is adamant about the need to educate youth regarding the dangers of prejudice, indifference, and inaction. I began to realize how important it is for me to do my part.

Inspired by Ursula, I have spent the last year and a half performing a variety of team-based service projects with AmeriCorps NCCC. I don't know the exact moment, but, during that year, I felt myself come alive. I encountered some of the most idealistic and passionate individuals I have ever met. We came from different parts of the country, were at different stages of our lives, and our futures were headed in different directions. But we shared the realization that we could not live with ourselves if we did not take this opportunity, while we still could, to help those around us. They brought out the best in me. Now in my second year with AmeriCorps, I work as a team leader and am responsible for the service experience of ten eighteen- to twenty-four-year-olds. It is more work than I ever imagined, but each day I have a sense of accomplishment.

In my time with AmeriCorps, I have primarily performed hands-on tasks, such as providing supplies with the Red Cross and repairing hurricane-damaged homes. As I performed these services, however, I came to realize that people require guidance in navigating the "system." As homeowners attempt to rebuild their homes after a disaster, they need help battling insurance companies that deny payments and contractors who cheat them. Like the parents of many of the elementary school students with whom my team now works, half of whom are currently homeless, people need assistance dealing with landlords and foreclosing banks as well as with government agencies that are sometimes insensitive to their needs. I have learned in the past year that lower income families need access to legal services. I believe that the best way I can serve is by becoming the finest attorney possible.

In American Samoa, community members came out to help one another more than in any community I have thus far visited. What I witnessed in the Samoan people was loyalty and a sense of responsibility to help one another. They were inspirational. I wish to follow their example and to demonstrate that it should not be out of the ordinary for a lawyer to devote her time to helping her fellow citizens. I plan to make public service a career. I want to help people help themselves—and then help one another.

Analysis

The powerful opening sentence catapults the reader headlong into the tsunami—an entrance that promises a vivid essay. Beginning in the middle of the action allows for the more dramatic and energizing introductions that are a hallmark of outstanding essays. Avery Hook's essay's initial burst engages because she knows how to tell a story. She drives the narrative with tsunami-fueled suspense. Yet at the same time, by the end of the first paragraph, she has already gestured to her relationships with the native Samoans and her impulse toward helping them.

Hook does an excellent job in narrowing her essay's subject so that it is neither so broad as to be unhelpful nor so limited as to be repetitive. Reading the vivid vignettes illuminates a formative aspect of her life that is not readily apparent from a formal résumé. Recounting her experiences rebuilding homes, delivering supplies, leading and learning from the Samoan population transplants the reader into her experience. She broadcasts the seriousness of her commitment to service, inspired by her interaction with Ursula that dangles a bit heavy-handedly in the middle of her essay, in order to effectively elucidate her motivations for pursuing law.

After the climactic rush of the anecdotal first paragraph, Hook transitions into more didactic writing. As a general rule, that should be kept to a minimum in personal statements, and it leaves the reader missing the essay's original strength of feeling. A phrase of commentary like "They were inspirational" risks feeling flat, especially next to her much more vivid recounting. Similar phrases, like "I felt myself come alive," feel weak beside the much realer palpitations of her experiences. Those phrases, paired with the brief, basic survey of families in need form a less-than-perfect bridge to the topic of law school motivation.

Still, Hook is making a successful case, and her experiences are her reasons, geared toward answering the question: Why does she want to attend Harvard Law School? Her conclusion needs her own words and commentary to fully provide an answer. Hook's final words—"I want to help people . . ."—might feel hackneyed if they stood alone. But her essay's stories—the supporting proofs—infuse that concluding promise with the sentiment she wants to impart.

—*Idrees Kahloon*

NICOLAS SANSONE

I have spent the last three years in a master's program for English at the University of Massachusetts, which has been simultaneously enriching and frustrating: enriching because I have been equipped with a variety of analytical lenses through which to view the social and historical implications of literary texts, and frustrating because I crave an opportunity to apply my interpretative skills to a discipline with a more immediate social impact. A career in international law is an opportunity to couple my aptitude for textual analysis with my desire to take active, concrete steps toward a more just world.

Throughout my education, I have focused on global inequalities. At Sarah Lawrence College, I studied heterodox economics, with a focus on the ways in which national policies shaped by adherence to the neoclassical model of capitalism have impaired equitable development both within and among countries. Puzzled and disheartened by the extremes of wealth and poverty I witnessed during a semester abroad in Moscow during my junior year, I was inspired to undertake a thesis paper for a macroeconomic theory and policy course I audited the following semester in which I attempted to understand this inequality through an analysis of Russia's transition to capitalism. The process of researching and developing this paper highlighted the ways in which flawed theory can result in flawed policy and, consequently, the importance of a consistent, logical, and humane theoretical foundation in ensuring social and economic justice.

In graduate school, too, I have been drawn to questions of international justice. In particular, I have gravitated toward postcolonial studies: the project of analyzing literary texts in light of their assumptions about national identity, cross-cultural exchange, and global capitalism. One of the texts I regularly elect to teach in my college writing classes is Jamaica Kincaid's *A Small Place*—an indictment of the role Antigua's colonial past has played in shaping its present dependence on an inequitable and exploitative tourist economy. My goal in teaching this essay is to inspire my students to think about the ways in which we passively reinforce historic injustices unless we actively fight against them.

Recently, however, I have been asking myself how I, personally, have worked to fight against global exploitation. I encourage my students to take up the battle, and I hope some of them will, but I have to admit that up to this point my approach to the questions of international justice has been purely academic. How can I take my students to task for being the passive beneficiaries of ongoing inequity when I myself have done nothing concrete to address it?

My inability to answer this question has been the primary motivation in my decision to apply to law school. Although global justice has consistently been one of my academic interests, it holds deep personal interest as well. As a lover of culture, landscape, and languages, I travel extensively and am therefore haunted by the figure of the tourist that Jamaica Kincaid's essay presents: a spoiled Westerner who blithely crosses international boundaries, heedless of his own position of privilege. I attempt to be sensitive to the impact I have on the places I visit, and I do remain aware of international events by reading *The Economist* and *The New York Review of Books*. Sensitivity and awareness alone, however, do nothing to address injustice: Concrete action is required as well.

The sort of concrete effort that will most satisfy me will take place at the level of policy. In the two years I spent working as a volunteer in the AmeriCorps National Civilian Community Corps, I experienced the satisfaction of direct, hands-on service in national forests, disaster zones, and low-income neighborhoods throughout the country. While immediate service work can go a long way toward alleviating individual instances of privation, however, it does not typically address the underlying structural roots that create and maintain social ills. I have been fortunate in my education and my volunteer experiences, but I am ready to take the necessary practical steps that will put me in a better position to engage directly with the social circumstances that generate and reinforce injustice.

I am entering the law school application process without the quixotic fantasy that I can single-handedly "save the world" over the course of a brief lifetime. However, although I don't know what the results of my anticipated involvement in international justice will be, I do know what the results of a failure to get involved would be: continued passive complicity with the *status quo* that has privileged me at others' expense. In light of this, I simply do not see how I can allow my interest in global affairs to remain exclusively academic.

Analysis

Nicolas Sansone quickly gets to the point in his application essay for Harvard Law. He states that he has spent the past three years in a master's program for English and how he now desires a way to apply his skills to "a discipline with a more immediate social impact." The rest of his essay explains why he views a career in international law as a way to benefit society and use his skills.

In his second and third paragraphs, Sansone explains how he has focused on global inequalities and matters of international justice in his undergraduate and graduate education respectively. He provides compelling examples of these experiences, such as his research of Russia's transition to capitalism and his teaching of Jamaica Kincaid's *A Small Place* to his college writing classes.

Sansone could have strengthened the essay if he had structured the essay more fluidly; perhaps he could have interwoven his academic achievements with his self-exploration and made both more compelling in the process. As it stands, the essay slips into résumé-imitating. Sansone jumps from a macroeconomics paper to his teaching to his time with AmeriCorps. He touches on important themes, but the examples he uses feel too forced at times to fully examine them.

The latter half of the essay is more personal, focusing on Sansone's self-exploration regarding how his work—or lack thereof—to fight global exploitation. The essay is strongest in these parts since his frank and self-aware style paint a portrait of the applicant. He admits that he is unable to answer the question "How can I take my students to task for being the passive beneficiaries of ongoing inequity when I myself have done nothing concrete to address it?" and is thus applying to law school. In admitting that he lacks perfection, that he doesn't hold all of the answers or experiences he needs—while showing that he does seek them—Sansone crafts a nuanced, thoughtful self-portrait. Ultimately, his sensitivity toward his lack of experience makes the essay an intriguing read.

—*Hayley Cuccinello*

ALENE GEORGIA ANELLO

The treatment of animals by our nation's industries is out of line with the public's sentiments about animal welfare. As a result, a revolution is taking place in animal law. States are enacting laws against cruel common business practices, such as harboring pregnant and nursing sows in crates too small to turn around. Meanwhile, in a backlash against animal welfare changes, states are also passing laws backed by the animal agriculture industry to stop activists from filming and exposing inhumane farm conditions.

I value my job at People for the Ethical Treatment of Animals (PETA), where I work to persuade Americans to make compassionate choices. Yet, when e-mails cross my inbox about exciting developments in the law to benefit animals, I yearn to participate in the legal process. I want to help ensure new animal welfare laws are enforced and upheld, to draft necessary legislation, and to defend the right to expose cruelty. My animal advocacy work so far has shown me that positive messages alone can often convince people to do right by animals, but I have come to believe that legal protection will ultimately help animals the most.

Ever since I rallied fellow sixth-graders to join a "Pigs Are Our Friends Not Our Food" club, I have been improving my skills to advocate for better treatment of animals. In high school, animal protection was a side interest. I was determined to help those in need, but I focused mainly on *people* in need. I led trips to serve meals to homeless people in New York City, worked with Mount Sinai School of Medicine researchers to study the causes of autism, volunteered on a child psychiatric ward, and canvassed for politicians who I thought would improve people's lives. In college, as I watched footage of the routine cruelty on factory farms and observed firsthand how easily people can improve animals' lives through relatively small changes, I was gradually drawn to focus on the cause of animal protection.

As a freshman, I helped convince Harvard University Dining Services to switch to about 50 percent cage-free eggs. (Harvard later went 100 percent cage-free.) I learned that, to foster change in a large institution, one must present information on public opinion, ethics, finances, and logistics. After this success, I was excited to help start the Harvard College Vegetarian Society, and eventually became its copresident. I invited vegetarian authors to speak at Harvard, showed films, and served free vegan meals. Hosting these events let me practice informative responses to questions about animal agriculture and vegan eating.

Coursework strengthened my conviction to work for animals: Neuroscience revealed to me the similarity between our brain and those of other species, and philosophy provided a framework to understand how a utilitarian concern for suffering leads to Bentham's argument that the law should protect animals. My classes also gave me tools with which to advocate for animals: Psychology taught me about persuasion, and portraiture taught me to foster understanding through images—a skill I practiced until my photos convinced an initially skeptical professor that animals could be the subjects of portraits.

For the past two years, at PETA, I have worked long hours to help create positive news events—such as PETA's Person of the Year awards given to Bill Clinton and Russell Simmons—that show Americans how simple choices can help animals. I train other PETA staff to do the same. My job has taught me to craft messages that interest reporters while also conveying important information to the public. In addition to my normal work, I regularly volunteer to address allegations of cruelty that are reported to PETA. Through this work, I have experienced the limits of current animal welfare laws, but I have also learned that a knowledgeable explanation may motivate law enforcement officials to respond to animal emergencies despite the limited legal arsenal available to them.

The books on persuasive communication that I read and reread, the lectures on advocacy that I seek out, and the discussions that I lead in my division's monthly meetings have helped me further refine my animal advocacy skills. I have learned to give positive reinforcement, to paint a vivid picture, and to emphasize common ground.

Now, I aim to gain new, more powerful, forums through which to advocate for animals, from the courtroom to the legislature, and to participate in the HLS Student Animal Legal Defense Fund so that I can continue to advance animal protection while I learn. I am eager to join and engage the Harvard Law School community.

Analysis

Every law school applicant understands the dint of their task before he or she makes moves to confront it—to succeed, he or she must offer the admissions officers a mirror into him/herself. The readers must not simply know facts about the life of the applicant; rather, they must understand the applicant, gaining insight into the candidate's passions and desires. Only then can they know with confidence that the author of the application essay is a true fit for their school.

Doing this successfully is not always the easiest to accomplish. It is common for an essayist to appear self-important or insincere in explaining how he or she reached this point in his or her life. The quality of Alene Georgia Anello's essay follows from the excellence in which its author avoids these traps, coming off as deeply genuine in adumbrating in detail how her life to date culminated in the desideration to attend one of the most prestigious law school in the country. This essay shows both the emotional tie Anello feels with the animal community and how she has seized every opportunity possible to do what is necessary to make the world a better place. Snippets like her reaction to videos of animal treatment get at the former; a concatenation of efforts from a sixth-grade rally to full-time work with PETA lay out the latter. At a young age, she identified a serious problem in the world around her, and she has worked tirelessly and passionately to eradicate that problem one step at a time. It is impossible to read this essay and not root for its author—to want to help her along to quench her insatiable search for righteousness.

That Anello evinces this feeling is a victory in and of itself, emboldened by the fact that her goals for attending law school are so clear in the essay. "I aim to gain new, more powerful, forums through which to advocate for animals, from the courtroom to the legislature," she makes clear, without equivocation. Anello has her passion, evinced by a long history of commitment to change. She does not want to go to HLS to "become a lawyer" or even for the hackneyed purpose of "making a difference." Yes, she wants to make a difference—but she knows exactly how she is going to do that, and why law school is such an important step in her grand design.

—*John F. M. Kocsis*

KHALEA ROSS ROBINSON

Two-Oh-Two-Seven-Two-Six-Five-Six-Two-Three. This string of numbers was the first I learned—to be recited on command for hypothetical firemen, the school nurse during pollen season, or both—and was delivered each time with a rapidity and enthusiasm that only a four-and-a-half-year-old could muster.

As trivial as this recollection may seem, the first three digits of the phone number I remember to this day as a jingle have meaning to me because of the place they represent—Washington, D.C. There, I was born to a mother on whose voice floated the gentle lilt of the West Indies, and a father whose baritone was as spiced with notes of the South as his seriousness was with laughter. The older I grew, the more faces the city showed me.

There was the Washington of polished heels through marble hallways. Of gavels, solemn and resolute, against sounding blocks. Of flag pins on the lapels of honorable gentlemen, and minced black truffle in salads at luncheons held in their honor.

There was also the Washington outside the hallways—outside the walls even. The Washington of handmade signs circling in front of the White House; soft, small hands and large, weathered ones alike, united by some shared belief, holding glowing candles pushed through Dixie cups to save well-meaning fingers from the ire of hot wax poised to fall.

But perhaps most noticeable, most dramatic, and most important to me, was the Washington that was not seen. The Washington, which did not have connections on the Hill, and did not have any real protest movement. The Washington that was promoted from grade to grade, all the way to cap and gown, stage and applause, and functional illiteracy. The Washington that barely had access to supermarkets, much less "power," but was affected in a very real way by each change to the housing, health care, and criminal justice policies that were drafted, voted on, and enacted with each new session. It was the invisible Washington that emptied the wastepaper baskets and polished the floors of the Washington that legislated, and that raked the leaves and shoveled the snow for the

Washington that marched. It was the Washington whose concerns were more vital than ideological. Its concerns were not even political—they were not even "new." They were, and are, as basic as equal sentencing for equal crimes.

While I never saw this Washington at school, I saw its daughters every Saturday morning—first at a public school for the arts, and then, once school administrators' congeniality had grown tired and our welcome worn thin, in the basement of a neighborhood church. Inside, forty figures, from seven to seventeen, would become one in the art and wonder of the arabesque and the pas de chat. And while a few of us studied in schools that were clearly preparing us for college, the vast majority of us did not.

Of all the mornings we spent there together, the memory most vivid in my mind is of the one Saturday that we spent neither stretching, at the barre, not *en pointe*, but rather kneeling on the floor: young girls with neat buns and bright eyes, leaning over newsprint, older ones helping younger ones, ballet slippers stuffed with newspaper to prevent creasing, all eagerly and meticulously spray-painting our light-pink ballet slippers a warm brown. All so that the visual seamlessness, which defines the art—the continuity of line, motion, and appearance from calf, to ankle, to pointed, slippered toe—could belong to the girls in that church basement also.

While I shall never forget the beauty of that moment—the resourcefulness and *innocence* of the girls on their knees that morning, carefully, faithfully fashioning for themselves slippers that no manufacturer thought to produce, it is my fervent hope that in their eventual maturity, they find their existence recognized; and that when they look to government as citizens, and to schools as parents, as they once looked to merchants as young dancers, they will find that—at last—they have been "seen." In the same way that a mastery of physics is essential to the design of a bridge that is to stand, I hope to master the law as the instrument with which to help ensure that in my first home—a city of confluence and contrast, adjacency and antithesis—these girls, its daughters, and the similarly forgotten, of all ages, genders, and ethnicities, are remembered.

Analysis

Khalea Ross Robinson's essay may be a "law school personal statement," but it is just as much a literary essay and effective because of it. From the digits intoned at the essay's opening to the anaphora of "the Washington" to the figurative and sweeping language at the essay's close, Robinson deploys her words carefully and with flair. In addition to improving the reader's experience, this carries some real weight: Robinson seeks entrance to a profession steeped in the written word.

Often, Robinson's literary approach enhances her thematic one. For instance, repeating "the Washington" reinforces the theme of the city and the different, insulated Washingtons it contains. Her vivid images, like that of the protesters and their weathered hands, convey thought and feeling. However, at times Robinson risks over-applying her literary verve. Her opening takes its time developing before launching to the essay's message. And with a consistent sequence of prose that borders on purple, Robinson dulls some of her most salient passages' effects. It's important to know when to speak artfully and when to deliver concision.

But Robinson doesn't simply show that she can craft her sentences. She shows that she can think. She carefully lays out the social problems and divisions she observes, and then relates them to her own experiences. Many essays treat injustice as a flat, uniform beast and make uncreative statements about commitment to defeating it. Robinson comes across as no less committed, but her use of imagery and her discernment offer a more balanced view that shows she has considered these issues in more than surface-level terms.

This case for admission to law school isn't explicit. The word "law" doesn't even appear until the final sentence. But you don't need to say "I want to go to law school" to say you want to go to law school. Instead, Robinson's essay incorporates a variety of elements that build her tacit case. Although this book files her essay under "Inspiration," a closer read reveals that a good personal statement like this can't be pigeonholed. Robinson shows she can write. She shows she can think. She presents the images and themes that have driven her progress from childhood to today. She relates a telling scene and links it to her own law school drive. This is an essay of evolution, storytelling, critical thinking, and yes, inspiration, wrapped up in one.

It's also an example of how what you write about and the way you write it interact to produce a total effect. So think about how you can fuse the techniques, strategies, and styles in this essay and the fifty-four others with the experiences and ideas you've amassed. Think about what a reader should glean from your few, brief pages. Think about how you can best display your own unique self. Then put it all together and complete the final step: write.

—*Brian Cronin*